Boot Up

Boot Up

The Daily Telegraph

BEGINNER'S GUIDE TO
COMPUTERS AND COMPUTING

Rick Maybury

TEXERE

LONDON · NEW YORK

First published in Great Britain in 1999 by
Orion Business

This edition published by

TEXERE Publishing Limited
71–77 Leadenhall Street
London
EC3A 3DE

Tel: +44 (0)20 7204 3644
Fax: +44 (0)20 7208 6701
www.texerepublishing.com

A subsidiary of

TEXERE LLC
55 East 52nd Street
New York, NY 10055

Tel: +1 (212) 317 5106
Fax: +1 (212) 317 5178

A CIP catalogue record for this book
is available from the British Library

ISBN 1–58799–052–0

Typeset by Selwood Systems, Midsomer Norton
Printed and bound in Great Britain by
Butler & Tanner Ltd, Frome and London

Contents

Introduction

How does the computer industry get away with it? In no other industry would people put up with the frankly dreadful standards that computer users take as read. When you buy a new car for example, you can reasonably expect it to work flawlessly for several years with minimum tinkering. Most of us never open the bonnet and, quite rightly, expect the annual service to see us through.

Not so the computer industry. When you buy a new machine you feel as if you need an A-level in computing just to switch it on. Computers must be the most capricious of all modern technology. One day they work fine, the next, for no obvious reason, they simply stop. You did nothing to them, you didn't go in and delete random files, pull out wires or tip coffee down the back. No, it just makes up its little silicon mind that today it's not going to switch on. Or even worse, it will switch on, but it won't do things in quite the same way as before.

And then there are the computer makers and software sellers. A deadly embrace keeps them feeding off each other. As technology gets cheaper, so computers get more powerful, so software makers eat up that extra computer power with 'extras'. Programs that once fitted on a single floppy disk, now come on twenty or more. And who benefits? Not the users who spend their lives having to buy more and more powerful computers just to stand still. A recent survey showed that most users use under 10 per cent of the features of software. Who really needs to be able to change the colour of the wiggly rule that underlines spelling mistakes? This is insanity.

It is time for the industry to wake up to the fact that typical users are not prepared to invest hours in trying to understand the language, learning their SYSBATs and their CONFIGs. What they want is a machine you can take out of the box, plug in and switch on. One that will work from Day One and still be working a year later. One that adapts to our needs, not one that forces us to adapt to its own. Instead of producing more and more bloated software, manufacturers should be producing more and more refined software. Software that treats us like humans; software that does what we want.

It would be churlish to say that the industry has ignored the public, for we have seen changes. Today's computers are much easier to use than those of say five years ago, but that says more about the journey, than the destination. We are moving in the right direction, but there is a long, long way to go yet.

For nearly three years, Connected has run a weekly column where we try to help people grapple with their computers; a sort of agony aunt for the digitally distressed. People who have invested the effort to penetrate the dense jungle of acronyms, abbreviations and jargon, but have fallen victim to the whims of their machines.

This was followed a year ago by Rick Maybury writing the Boot Camp series to help people who were getting to grips with computers for the first time. This book combines this accumulated advice for anyone who is more interested in actually using their computer than in trying to decipher its manual.

Existing computer books seem to fall into two camps. They are either patronising, assuming you are a 'dummy' or an 'idiot', or they are simply baffling. So too with so many magazines. They are written in a language seemingly designed to exclude not explain. In a clear, easy to understand style, *Boot Up* explains how you can get the most from your machine. Jargon is avoided but any essential terms are marked in bold in the text and explained in the glossary.

One day books like this will be unnecessary. You don't buy a guide to operate your TV, or one on how to drive a car. Until we reach that digital nirvana, we need all the help we can get. A lot of that help is in these pages.

Ben Rooney
Editor
Connected, *The Daily Telegraph*

CHAPTER 1 **Buying a PC**

You've decided to buy a PC, but where do you start? Let's begin with the basics. And a few home truths ...

Frustration is something PC owners quickly become accustomed to, and that's long before the inevitable software crashes or inexplicable error messages appear on the screen. Within weeks of buying a new PC you can be fairly sure you'll see the same, or a similarly specified model selling for significantly less than you paid for it; within five years it will be practically worthless. There is never a right time to buy a PC. If you want one buy it now. Get the fastest, most powerful machine you can afford and resign yourself to the fact that it will be effectively obsolete before you get it home and out of the box.

That might sound a bit bleak, but it's not meant to be. The modern PC has to be the bargain of the century. What other product doubles in performance yet halves in price every couple of years? Even though most PCs are technically outmoded before they reach the end of the production line, you can expect to get at least four or five years of service out of an up-to-date model, if you're using it for routine applications like word processing and financial planning. Most PCs can be upgraded to extend their useful working lives, or adapt to newly developed software or peripherals, so what should you be looking for?

For the sake of simplicity we'll concentrate on computers using the Windows operating system, which is currently used on over 90% of the world's PCs. There are alternatives, notably Apple Macintosh systems, and there is much to commend them, but Windows PCs still represent the best value and provide the greatest flexibility for the vast majority of home and business users.

Inside a PC there are three critical components that ultimately determine performance and useful working life. They are the central processor chip, the amount of **RAM** (Random Access Memory), and the size of the PC's hard disk drive.

Virtually all new machines use the Intel Pentium chip, or one of its many equivalents, made by companies such as AMD, Cyrix and IBM. Until fairly recently Pentium and Pentium-class processor chips were more or less interchangeable in terms of performance and capability but Intel have introduced a new generation of processor chips, called Pentium II. Other manufacturers are fast fighting back with improved versions of their existing processor chips and while the Intel brand has the highest profile, rival chip-makers offer comparable performance, often at significantly lower prices.

Processor speed – i.e. how quickly the chip carries out calculations – is measured in megahertz (MHz), and you can take it as read that the bigger the number, the better. The current norm is from 233MHz to 400MHz, which is fast enough for all but the most demanding applications. By all means go for a faster machine, but it won't make a great deal of difference to most existing programs; if the need arises for a faster machine you can always replace the processor chip. You will probably see the letters MMX after the processor speed in a lot of advertisements. This stands for Multi-Media eXtensions, and basically indicates that the processor chip is good for playing games.

Deciding how much **RAM** capacity you need is easy. Do not buy a PC with less than 32Mb (megabytes) of **RAM**, but you really should be aiming for at least 64Mb, and since memory microchips are relatively cheap, it won't add significantly to the price. You may come across a reference to **cache** memory – this helps make the computer run faster, and a figure of 512Kb (kilobytes) is fairly standard. Most manufacturers will also mention video memory. As usual the bigger the better as it will improve the look of games and multimedia applications. 2Mb is fairly common, but if you get a choice, and are likely to be playing a lot of games, opt for 4Mb and one of the so-called '3D' graphics cards or accelerators.

Hard disk drive capacity is another reasonably simple matter. A 4.3Gb (gigabyte) drive is the absolute minimum. However, even that could prove insufficient in one or two years' time, as new, heavyweight applications written for the Windows 98 **operating system** reach the market. To be on the safe side opt for machines with 8.4Gb drives, unless you are on a very tight budget and unlikely to be handling a lot of large graphics or video files.

Now we come to the ancillaries. Almost all new PCs come with a 15-inch monitor but a 17-inch screen is better, and usually adds little to the package price. However, be aware that they do take up quite a bit more desk space. CD-ROM drives are a more or less standard fitting; some companies are now offering newer DVD-ROM drives as an alternative. It's a worthwhile option as **DVD** is likely to become the *de-facto* standard for software distribution in the next few years. All **DVD** drives can read CD-ROM disks, so there's no need to worry about compatibility. Built-in **modems** are also increasingly common – look for the speed rating, which should be either 33,600 (33K) or 56,000 (56K) bits per second (bps). Anything less simply will not do!

All PCs come with a keyboard and mouse but the quality of the standard offerings varies enormously. It is worth trying to negotiate an upgrade to better made products or ergonomic alternatives, particularly if you are going to be doing a lot of typing or have any type of disability in your fingers or wrists that could be aggravated by cheap input and pointing devices. Always try before you buy.

You can expect a new PC to come with the Windows **operating system** pre-loaded. This is likely to be the Windows 98 version, though a lot of suppliers can still provide Windows 95, if that's what you prefer. Generally speaking, Windows 98 is the best bet on a new machine as it has a number of future-proofing features and improved trouble-shooting facilities. Make sure that you receive the original software installation disk on CD-ROM and any other disks that may be required.

PC hardware is pretty reliable these days – most of the trouble is caused by software. Even so, you can of course expect to suffer a few teething troubles. Make sure the supplier or dealer offers a free telephone support service at the very least, and carefully check the conditions of the warranty. Finally, ask the salesperson to explain the ins and outs of their on-site or return-to-base servicing facilities, and if you decide to place an order, insist on a written copy of all the details, and a firm delivery date. If possible pay by credit card as this will give you the most protection, should anything go wrong.

Q&A   Solving Real World Problems

Build or buy?

Q   I am a student at university and would like to buy a PC with multi-media capability. I was thinking of buying the components and building it myself, but as far as I can see this wouldn't save me a lot of money. However, the university computer lab technician – a very wise man – says that you can save up to 40% this way.
S.H. via e-mail

A   That kind of saving might just have been possible four or five years ago, but not any more. Companies putting together PCs have tremendous buying power, and there's intense competition, so high street prices are very low. You might be able to save a few pounds, building a machine from off-the-shelf components – even at current retail prices – but you couldn't match the kind of package deals that include several hundred pounds' worth of software, or peripherals like printers and digital cameras.

Ready-built machines also come with a guarantee and some sort of service backup – though that can be a mixed blessing. They've usually been soak-tested (where the new machine is run continually for twenty-four hours in order to weed out any early failures) and the operating system should be pre-installed. That's not to say building a PC isn't a worthwhile exercise. It is, particularly if you can scavenge some parts to keep the cost down. Cases and power supplies, keyboards, mice and monitors can usually be safely recycled. It's not difficult and you get the exact specification that you require. It can be very rewarding, especially if it works first time; if it doesn't, you'll have the opportunity to learn all about PC fault-finding. If you're determined to go ahead, there are several books on the subject worth perusing first, including *Building Your Own PC* by A. Lee (Abacus Software), *Build Your Own Pentium Processor PC* by Aubrey Pilgrim (McGraw-Hill) and *Build Your Own Computer* by K. Hughes (Wordware Publishing). They are available from computer stores, or you can order them via the Internet from companies like Computer Manual Ltd at http://www.compman.co.uk

Wet vet

Q   I operate a veterinary practice in rural North Wales and use a PC at the surgery for record keeping etc. I also need to keep a lot of information on a laptop, but to date I've trashed three of them, either through getting bashed around in the back of the Land Rover, or in one case, falling into a slurry pit. Do you know of a portable PC that could survive this kind of rough treatment?
D.R.T. via e-mail

A   Husky Computers produce a number of 'ruggedised' portable IBM compatible PCs. They're built to a military specification, and can withstand a drop of 1.5 metres onto a solid surface. They're also waterproof and will operate in temperatures from –20 to +60°C. Various levels of specification are available and prices start at under £2,000. For more details contact Husky Computers Ltd on 01203 604040 or at www.wpihusky.com

Shop or post?

Q   The price of PCs bought by mail order seems to be significantly less than those bought on the high street. What's the catch?
P.M. via e-mail

A   There isn't one. Mail order firms have lower overheads and usually build PCs to order whereas a shop has to maintain large stocks and employ sales staff. The only real difference is that you are buying the product unseen, and it lacks the personal touch. In virtually all other respects, including maintenance and after-sales backup there's little to choose between the two markets these days.

Colour bar

Q   Why do all computers seem to be the same colour? Maybe PC users do not want the same lurid colours as other products but there does seem to be an element of any colour you want, as long as it's off-white.
M.S. Oxford

A   It goes back to the days when computers were items of office equipment and rarely found in the home. Several manufacturers have tried marketing 'living-room' PCs, housed in black and slate-grey boxes, presumably to match the cosmetics of hi-fis, TVs and VCRs, but cream or off-white remains the colour of choice. If you're bored with manufacturer's schemes there's nothing to stop you whipping the lid off the box and spraying the outside using a tin of car paint. There's clearly a market for enterprising cabinet-makers and artists to produce custom finishes.

Screen size

Q   What would you consider to be the optimum screen size for a home PC, based on the fact that it will be mainly used for word processing and home finance programs and possibly the odd game?
L.L. Sussex

A   Until fairly recently most new PCs came with 14-inch monitors, though bear in mind this is a diagonal measurement of the picture tube, and not the visible screen area. The current norm is 15-inches, (12.5 to 13 inches visible) and this is about right for most applications. It's only worth thinking about a larger screen (17 to 19 inches) if you're going to be using it for a lot of graphics based applications and serious gaming, and if you have plenty of space – larger monitors take up a lot of room!

Warranted expense

Q   What do you think about extended warranty schemes for computers? Are they worthwhile?
M.K. Edinburgh

A   It depends. PCs are becoming more reliable and since they're based on modular construction, repairs can be fast and relatively inexpensive; most of the components inside a typical PC cost less than £100. They're worth considering if you want peace of mind, though do check to make sure the scheme includes same-day on-site maintenance. Bear in mind also that the price of a PC is falling all the time and the cost of a five-year warranty, say, may well exceed the value of your machine in a few years' time.

Flat spin ...

Q   I am considering buying a new 14-inch monitor for my PC. Can you tell me if the new 'flat screen' LCD displays are any good, and whether or not they justify the extra cost?
L.S. Essex

A   LCD monitors are expensive – currently about seven or eight times as much as a normal cathode ray tube (CRT) monitor, of equivalent screen size. Performance isn't as good either, colour fidelity and contrast are inferior to CRT-based monitors, and they have a shallower viewing angle. In their favour they take up a lot less desk space, power consumption is a lot lower, and they do not emit any harmful radiation. Prices will fall, but it will probably be a while before flat screen monitors are a mainstream computer peripheral.

Parity check

Q   I'm about to upgrade the memory on my PC but I'm confused about 'parity'. What is it, and do I need to be concerned about it?
D.E.S. Lakenheath

A   Parity is the means by which some memory modules (**SIMM** or single in-line memory module) check the integrity of the date they're storing. Briefly, an extra data bit is added to each byte of data passing in and out of the **SIMM**, indicating whether or not the 'number' is valid. If your machine is set up to use parity check, then you have to upgrade using **SIMMs** of the same type, if not you can use either parity or non-parity memory. You may be able to tell which sort you have by counting the number of chips on the memory modules. If there are 8 chips per module then they're almost certainly non-parity **SIMMs**, 9 chips invariably means the boards have parity. If you are unsure about the type of memory you need, you should consult the dealer, or take your machine along to have it fitted by an engineer.

Brand loyalty

Q   Is there much difference between one internal **modem** and another? I notice that many manufacturers ship machines with unbranded **modems**, so one has to assume that these devices are perfectly adequate, yet the difference in price between branded and unbranded is enormous. Which should I go for?
T.N. via e-mail

A   A lot of internal **modems** are actually made by the same companies, and use the same chips, as products from the better-known brands. After-sales support for unbranded **modems** can be patchy or non-existent, they may lack some more advanced features, or come with different software packages, but in our experience there's comparatively little variation in performance between most **modems** operating at speeds up to 33.6 kbps (kilobits per second).

Latest best?

Q   Do I really need to buy the latest whizzo PC? What's wrong with slightly older models? They seem to be a lot cheaper.
A.D. via e-mail

A   If you only want a PC for word processing and Internet connection then there's nothing wrong at all with older Pentium machines although earlier models using pre-Pentium '386' and '486' processor chips are getting a bit past it. Super-fast PCs are only really necessary if you want to keep up with the games market or if you are planning to use a lot of intensive graphics-based applications.

CHAPTER 2

Getting to know you – the multimedia PC

You've unpacked your gleaming multimedia computer. What now? Follow us on a guided tour of the main box, and don't worry about that mass of cables and sockets ...

Unlike most other electronic devices and appliances, PCs retain an air of mystery. The functions of the monitor, keyboard, mouse and loudspeakers are all fairly obvious, but the big cream-coloured box or 'system unit' – which they all plug into – gives little away. It's not necessary to understand how a PC works in order to use one, but it helps to know a bit about what's inside. The chances are that sooner or later you will want to remove the lid, to carry out an upgrade, add extra functionality, or try to find out why it has stopped working.

The heart of any PC is the **motherboard**. This large printed circuit board, mounted on the side or the bottom of the case, contains the central processing unit (CPU). This is the main microprocessor chip that does all the calculations. Older PC processors were known by a number designation – 80086, 80286, 80386, 80486 – but chipmakers Intel have started giving them names, Pentium and Celeron being the best known. The **motherboard** also contains all of the support systems for the CPU and the other components inside the case. The CPU is the biggest chip on the board, often fitted with a finned metal heat sink and miniature cooling fan. Some CPUs are mounted in a clamp or **ZIF** socket, so they can be easily removed. Pentium II processors are housed inside a black box that bolts to a socket on the **motherboard**.

The next most important area of the **motherboard** is the rows of memory sockets; some or all of them will be populated with memory boards. These are small strips or circuit boards, a couple of centimetres

The basic components of your home computer

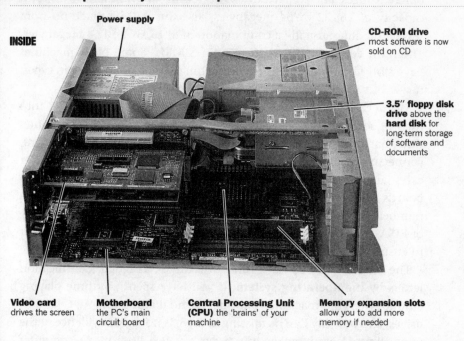

INSIDE

Power supply

CD-ROM drive
most software is now
sold on CD

**3.5″ floppy disk
drive** above the
hard disk for
long-term storage
of software and
documents

Video card
drives the screen

Motherboard
the PC's main
circuit board

**Central Processing Unit
(CPU)** the 'brains' of your
machine

Memory expansion slots
allow you to add more
memory if needed

BACK VIEW

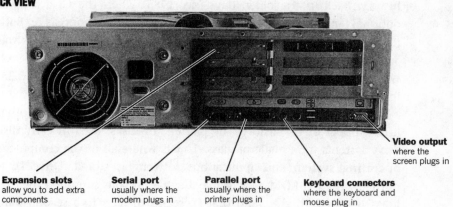

Video output
where the
screen plugs in

Expansion slots
allow you to add extra
components

Serial port
usually where the
modem plugs in

Parallel port
usually where the
printer plugs in

Keyboard connectors
where the keyboard and
mouse plug in

The basic components of your home computer

wide, with **RAM** chips on one or both sides which come in several different sizes and capacities. Most recent machines have a **RAM** capacity of 16, 32 or 64 megabytes, and this will be made up from several modules, usually a combination of 8, 16, 32 and 64 megabytes. The most common size is the 72-pin **SIMMs**. Some older machines have slots for 30-pin **SIMMs**, or a combination of 30 and 72-pin types; newer PCs mostly use 168-pin **DIMMs**.

Motherboards have a number of 'daughterboards' that plug into rows of sockets or 'expansion slots'. These may include the graphics card that processes the video output for the monitor, a sound card, connected to the speakers, controller cards for disk drives and other external devices and possibly an internal **modem**. Recent **motherboards** may have some or all of these functions built in. There are a number of different types of expansion slot; most PCs have a mixture of **EISA/ISA** and **PCI** sockets. When adding a new card it's important to ensure that there is a vacant slot of the correct type.

The majority of PCs have three disk drives, assigned identification letters by the **operating system**. If you have spent any time playing around with your machine you will have no doubt found A:, C: and D: drives, and possibly E:. The missing B: drive is not more evidence of the imbecility of computer manufacturers – it is a little bit of computer history. Back in the olden days (say 1985) when the C: drive was optional (and expensive), B: drives were almost as common as A:. Both refer to removable or floppy disks. At that time the standard disk was 5.25 inches across and flexible (i.e. floppy). When the current 3.5-inch type disk arrived it took over from the A: drive, leaving B: for the 5.25-inch disks. These have long since disappeared.

Drive C: is the main hard disk drive. The name hard drive is another little snippet of PC history; the platters, or disks, used in early disk drive systems were made of glass. This is where all of the computer's **operating system** and applications software is stored. Drive D: is normally the CD-ROM deck. It may be that on your computer the CD-ROM is called drive E:, and that D: seems to refer to a second hard drive. If so this simply means that your hard disk has been divided up or partitioned (logically, not physically of course) and is treated by the machine as two separate disks.

The power supply module is housed in a metal case with a built-in cooling fan. All PCs have an internal speaker that bleeps at you when you switch on or 'boot up'. One or two bleeps usually means all's well, if you hear any more then it may indicate there's a problem.

On the back panel of a PC you will find a rash of plugs and sockets, known as communication 'ports'. Why manufacturers insist on sticking these around the back is a mystery. It is very inconvenient, especially when it comes to plugging and unplugging external devices or peripherals.

There are normally two serial communication ports, COM 1 – a small round socket or 9-pin connector – is generally used by the mouse. COM 2 (9 or 25 pins) connects to external devices, like a **modem** or a digital camera. The 25-pin parallel port, designated LPT 1, is used by the printer and shared with other peripherals, such as scanners and external disk drives. The monitor cable also plugs into a 15-pin socket, on the back of the graphics card. A deeply recessed round socket is for the keyboard and there may be several jack sockets, for the loudspeakers and a microphone. Although plugs and sockets are not always marked, it should be clear where each cable goes, and impossible – in theory – to mix them up.

Q&A Solutions to real world problems

Universal solution

Q   My PC has two **USB** ports. What are they, and what do they do?
N.H. Cardiff

A   **USB** stands for Universal Serial Bus which is a newly standardised high-speed serial port for PC peripherals, like printers, scanners and cameras. It has a number of advantages: up to 127 devices can be 'daisy-chained' to a single connector; they can be plugged in whilst the PC is running; and there should be no need to change any of the PC's configuration settings. It's very early days for **USB** and at the moment only a handful of **USB** products have reached the marketplace.

TV connection

Q   Can I connect my PC to my television? I would like to use a larger screen, but the cost of large screen monitors is prohibitive.
T.D. via e-mail

A   A small handful of PCs have video outputs as standard that are suitable for connection to a TV, but in general you will need to buy a PC to TV adapter card, which has to be fitted inside the machine. External adapters are also available, which connect to the monitor output socket. In general, however, domestic TVs produce an inferior picture to a monitor, with reduced resolution and increased screen flicker, and are really only suitable for games. The other alternative is a TV with a PC VGA (video graphics array) input; several top-end models now have this facility, though again, the picture is not as good as a pukka monitor.

Head start

Q   Can I plug headphones instead of speakers into my PC, so I can play games without disturbing others?
P.P. Norwich

A   You can, but be very careful with the volume setting as on some models it can exceed the power handling capabilities of the headphones. You can also plug headphones into most CD-ROM drives, so you can listen to audio CDs.

Ports of call

Q   I know this might seem like an elementary question, but with regard to the equipment you mention, i.e. scanners, **zip** drives etc., do these items involve the installation of cards apart from the software? To which port is the hardware connected?
A.L. via e-mail

A   The majority of budget and mid-range flatbed scanners use a **SCSI** (small computer system interface) card, known as 'scuzzy' to its friends

– and enemies. The card plugs into a spare **ISA** expansion socket inside the machine. Some models now come with **PCI SCSI** cards, which improve performance dramatically. A few scanners connect to the PC's parallel printer port; these have a bypass connection, so the printer can remain connected. **Zip** drives are available with parallel port or **SCSI** card interfaces. Faster, higher capacity external drives like the Iomega Jazz are usually **SCSI** only. Devices like digital video cameras generally connect to one of the PC's serial ports.

Serial slowdown

Q I have managed to connect my desktop PC to my laptop using Windows 95 Direct Cable Connection, via the serial ports. Although everything is working correctly, the link is very slow. When I copied a large file from one to the other, I estimated the speed was probably 9,600 bps. I've tried changing the properties on the COM ports on both computers but this has no effect. Is there a way to speed things up?
R.V. via e-mail

A There is. You should change from a serial to a parallel connection – a suitable cable can be obtained from your local PC dealer for about £10. The general advice is to only use a serial cable if the parallel printer ports on the two PCs are unavailable for some reason. The fastest possible data transfer speeds will be obtained when both machines have an ECP (extended capabilities port) connection, but check to ensure the option has been enabled in your computer's **BIOS** set-up program. The procedure should be outlined in the instruction manuals.

Leading question

Q What is the longest lead I can use to connect my PC to a printer?
S.L. via e-mail

A The maximum recommended length for a parallel printer cable is five metres, though in practice you can get away with six or seven metres, assuming you're using good quality cables.

Mobile monitor

Q I keep my computer in my study but quite often I would like to work in a different room, or even in the garden. What is the longest lead I can use with the monitor and keyboard, so that I could move them but leave the computer undisturbed?
J.P. via e-mail

A You would have to provide a mains supply for the monitor, and an extension cable for the mouse as well, but increasing the length of any of the leads connecting the various devices attached to your PC is not advisable. The data and picture signals passing through these cables are very weak. Increasing the cable lengths by more than a few metres would weaken them still further and render them liable to interference and corruption. The only viable alternative is a second PC, have you thought about a laptop? Basic models, suitable for word processing and similar routine applications can be bought for less than £500. You might even consider a palmtop PC, though the keyboards on most models are rather small and not conducive to fast typing.

Key question

Q A lot of PCs have what appears to be a keyhole on the front panel. What is it for?
P.D. Derby

A It's a keyboard lock, designed to immobilise the keyboard and prevent the PC from being used. This feature is fast disappearing as it's easily overridden. Software security programs are much harder to crack.

Flying by wire?

Q I have problems running *Flight Simulator 98* on my ageing 486. It runs perfectly on my recently purchased laptop PC though, but the screen is too small to see the controls clearly – necessary when flying a Jumbo Jet... I think there must be a way of using the larger monitor on my PC

in conjunction with the power of my laptop. I've tried with Laplink on 'remote' but it still uses the PC system. Any suggestions? I've crashed three Jumbos and a Cessna already!
D.C. via e-mail

A   Virtually all notebook and portable PCs have a VGA socket, which will allow you to connect them to a PC monitor, using a standard cable. Some models also have a TV output as well, though you may find that the display quality is not sharp or stable enough for text-based applications, though it should be okay for games and simulation software. You should also be able to use a higher resolution setting than the LCD screen would normally permit. This facility can be found in Control Panel – double click on the Display icon and choose the Settings tab.

Turbo charge

Q   My first PC had a turbo button and while I was never quite sure what it did, I've noticed that new PCs don't seem to have them any more. Why?
E.M.L. via e-mail

A   The turbo feature was actually a way of slowing early PCs down, so they could run certain programs. They're not needed any more and modern PCs are designed to operate at their optimum speed, all of the time.

CHAPTER 3

A date with your desktop

*Say hello to Windows 95, the 'front end' of your
PC – it's the main link between you and your
computer. Don't worry, it's not as daunting as it
looks ...*

If you have recently come face to face with Windows 95 (or 98) for the
first time, you may not believe it, but computers used to be really
difficult to use. When the first office computers began to appear in the
late 1970s, operators required extensive training in order to use them.
Programs, such as word processors, interacted with the computer using
a relatively simply disk operating system or **DOS**. Computer users had
to learn scores of **DOS** command lines. They were obscure abbreviations that made the program carry out a particular function and in
addition a lot of operations used the 'Function' keys along the top edge
of the keyboard.

That's all history now (though the Function keys remain). Modern PCs
use a graphical user interface or GUI (pronounced 'gooey'), with little
pictures or icons on a sort of virtual on-screen desktop, representing
various functions and programs. The first GUIs were used by Apple
Macintosh in the early 1980s, and for several years Macs were sought after
because they were so easy to use. Microsoft developed the first version of
their 'Windows' **operating system** in 1984, but it wasn't a great success
and serious PC users continued to use **DOS** programs, while those looking
for an easier solution bought Macs. Then, in 1990 Microsoft released
version 3 of Windows. It was a major advance on previous operating
systems, and it gave the PC market an enormous boost. Windows 3 is still
in widespread use but it was officially superseded in 1995, with the launch
of Windows 95, and more recently updated with Windows 98, though the
move from Windows 95 to 98 is a far less radical change, than was the
move from Windows 3 to Windows 95.

The opening display on Windows 95 and 98 is known as the 'desktop'. The metaphor is well chosen; on a new Windows 95 PC the first thing you see – after it has finished booting up – is an almost empty work space, with just a handful of icons. Remember it well, for it quickly fills up as you load new software and create files. Soon it will start to look like a real office desk, cluttered and covered with things that you don't use or no longer need. Even though there's only a few icons to start with, newcomers often want to know if they can get rid of the ones they don't use, need or understand. The best advice is to leave well alone, for the moment. In any case, Windows 95 won't let you delete any icons it installed, at least not without a struggle.

There are two desktop icons that you should get to know straight away, which are My Computer, and the Recycle Bin. My Computer is a way to navigate and examine the various bits of hardware and software installed on your PC. Recycle Bin is a real lifesaver – should you ever delete anything by accident (and rest assured you will), Windows 95 can restore files from the Recycle Bin, even whole programs, but only if it hasn't been emptied recently!

The purpose of the Inbox, Microsoft Network and The Internet icons will become apparent if you sign up for Internet access, via Windows 95. Inbox is where your e-mail messages end up. The Internet and Microsoft Network are ways of automatically signing up an Internet account and then using it. However, don't rush into anything. Shop around and seek advice from seasoned net users. Laptop owners with Windows 95 machines will encounter an icon called My Briefcase. This is used to update files on a desktop PC when it is connected to the laptop by cable, network or Internet link.

Desktop icons are a quick way to access frequently used programs when a PC is first switched on, but far and away the most useful feature on the desktop is the Start button and Taskbar. However, it takes up valuable screen space, so one of the first things you can do is to make it disappear, until you need it. That option can be found in Settings; after clicking on the Start button, select Taskbar and check Auto-hide. After that the Start button and Taskbar will only appear when the mouse pointer goes to the bottom of the screen. If you prefer, you can move it to the top or sides of the screen, by clicking on the Taskbar, and dragging it to where you want it to be.

All of the software installed on your computer can be found listed under Programs on the Start menu and here you will find another very handy utility called Windows Explorer. Like My Computer it's a useful way of moving around inside directories, folders and files on your machine. When you double click on the Explorer icon you will see all of the files and folders listed on what's known as a 'tree'. Most folders have a little plus sign next to them, which when clicked on will open the folder, to show you what is inside. There you may find files, or possibly more folders, which in turn can be opened to reveal the contents, thus expanding another 'branch' of the tree.

The Windows desktop and Control Panel, a collection of utilities for customising the way your PC looks and performs

The Control Panel in the Settings option is an important feature of Windows 95; it is crammed full of icons that determine how the PC behaves. A good way of getting to know your machine is to customise a few settings. Start with Display, which will allow you to play around with colour schemes and screen savers but avoid changing anything on the Settings tab until you're a little more experienced. Help, on the Start menu is an invaluable resource. Get to know it, and how it works as it's a veritable fount of wisdom. You will find most of the answers to your questions there, and it is a whole lot cheaper than manufacturers' Helplines.

Q&A   Solutions to real world problems

On the button

Q   Most new PCs nowadays seem to come with a 'Windows 95' keyboard. I've recently upgraded my software to Windows 95, do I need the keyboard as well?
O.Y. Nuneaton

A   Not at all, the main difference is the addition of the Windows key, which operates the Start button – you can achieve the same effect on any ordinary keyboard by pressing the Ctrl + Escape keys.

Wandering start

Q   My wife and I have a brand new Pentium PC with Windows 95 installed. When new, the Start button was in the bottom left hand corner of the screen. It later moved to the other side. No one can explain to me how it got there – have you any ideas? It is doing no harm there so I am not asking how to restore it to its original location.
L.T. via e-mail

A   It's unlikely the Start button and Taskbar moved of its own accord. It can be positioned on any one of the four sides of the screen, simply by moving the mouse pointer onto a vacant part of the Taskbar, clicking and holding, then dragging it to where you want it to go. It's quite easy to do it unintentionally, which is probably what happened in your case. One way to prevent it reoccurring, and to free up some screen space, is to make the Start button and Taskbar disappear, until they're needed. You can enable this option by clicking on Settings on the Start menu, selecting Taskbar, and checking the Auto Hide box. The Start button will then only appear when the mouse pointer moves to the part of the screen where it has been placed.

Mobile icons

Q   The icons on my desktop seem to have minds of their own. How can I make sure they stay put, instead of wandering around all over the place?
R.J. via e-mail

A   Right click your mouse on an empty area of the desktop, select Arrange Icons, and then click on the Auto Arrange option and they will be neatly stacked in rows.

Stop start

Q   I have a Pentium 120 with Windows 95. When I switch on my computer my desktop gets layered with windows, which ask me if I want to run certain programs. I have managed to get rid of some of them because they had check boxes, which if ticked will not load next time. However, others don't have this option and I end up having to click cancel boxes every time I switch on my computer. I even get four belonging to the same program asking me if I want to connect to the Internet. How do I stop these from loading every time I switch on?
P.R.W. via e-mail

A   You need to edit your PC's start-up folder. This can be found by clicking on the Start button, then Settings, select Taskbar and the Start Menu Programs tab. Click the Remove button and scroll down the list of folders until you come to one called StartUp. Double click on the '+' sign to show the contents, highlight the programs you do not want to start automatically then click Remove.

Wrong icons

Q   The desktop icons for My Computer and Recycle Bin have changed to the Windows icon. Is there a way of reinstating them to their original form?
M.G. via e-mail

A   You need to get hold of a small utility program called TweakUI, which has an Icon Reconstruction option, and much more besides. It is part of the PowerToys package and can be downloaded from the Microsoft web site and is regularly featured on computer magazine cover-mounted CD-ROMs. Alternatively find it at http://www.microsoft.com/windows/download/powertoy.exe

Screen gems

Q   I have made several unsuccessful and frustrating attempts to create my own screen saver, from a scanned colour picture. However, when I go into Display and then the Screen Saver menu, there is no command that allows me to import it. I would very much appreciate it if you could talk me through the process.
R.M. via e-mail

A   The main purpose of a screen saver is to prevent phosphor 'burn', caused by a static image remaining on the screen for hours on end. In other words, to be effective a screen saver should constantly change or move. As it stands, your static scanned photograph would be unsuitable as a screen saver; indeed, it could even cause screen burn. A simple little **shareware** utility called 'Make Your Own Screen Saver', from Preferred Computer Services is worth a try. Once installed it operates from the Screen Saver tab on the Display icon in Control Panel. Simply choose your image and it's instantly transformed into a moving screen saver. There are more than a dozen display options, including float, wipe, zoom and blocks. You can find Preferred Computer Services at http://www.customsavers.com/download.htm

Passing clouds

Q   It is bad enough waiting for my PC to switch itself off, without having to stare at that really annoying picture of clouds and the patronising 'it is now safe...' message at the end. Can they be removed or replaced?
A.J. Cheshire

A   It's quite easy to modify or change the sign-off graphics, which are basically simple bitmap (BMP) files. You'll find them in the main Windows 95 directory. They're called logos.sys and logow.sys and you can look for them in Explorer – they're down past all the yellow folders. If you want to have a fiddle around, open the Paint utility in Accessories (or your preferred graphics program). Click on Open in the File menu. Open the Windows folder, change the type of file field to All Files, and they should appear.

You can do anything you like to the images – add extra text or your own freehand graphics and colours, then save them, and that's what you'll see next time you switch off. You can even create your own, though any image must conform to strict parameters and be configured as a 320 × 400 pixel, 256-colour bitmap.

If you can't find logo.sys in the Windows directory, the machine is using a version that is embedded in a file called io.sys, also in the C:\directory. The trouble is you can't easily get at it. Fortunately any file called logo.sys placed in the root directory will override the one in io.sys.

Getting the point

Q   I used to have a red coloured mouse pointer, which I found very helpful. I upgraded to Windows 95 and the pointer is now black, but I cannot find how to turn it red again.
D.P. via fax

A   Pointer options in Windows 95 are rather limited, and there's no easy way to change the colour. Incidentally, pointers and the hourglass live in a file called 'cursors'; you'll find it in the Windows directory. Your best bet is to get hold of an Icon Editor program. Microangelo from Impact Software is well worth trying – you can use it to change the shape, colour and look of your pointers and desktop icons, and you can even design new ones. A trial version is available from their web site for the cost of a three-minute download. It also turns up on magazine cover disks from time to time. Microangelo can be found at: http://www.impactsoft.com/muangelo/download/ma21.**zip**

Pass friend

Q   At start up the Enter Windows Password box appears, prompting me for User Name and Password. I have tried the OK option, but it will only allow me to use the Cancel option. What have I done? Is there a cure?
M.G. via e-mail

A   At some point you, or someone else has selected the password option, which allows several people to configure Windows 95 to their own personal preferences. You can switch it off by opening Control panel from the Start menu, and clicking on the Password icon. Select the 'All users of this PC...' option, then click on OK.

If that doesn't work try this. From the Start Menu select Find and in the 'Named' field type '*.PWL' (without the inverted commas of course), and click on Find Now. You should find one or more of these files in the Windows folder, they contain your password data (and that of anyone else who uses the machine). Simply delete or rename the files (*.OLD, or something similar), then restart the computer. When the password box next appears put in your user name but leave the password field blank, and press Enter. When you next restart the computer the password box should hopefully be no more.

Dodgy diagnosis

Q   About a year ago I bought what I was led to believe is a 75MHz Pentium PC, running Windows 95. A few days ago I came across the MSD utility in **DOS**, which reported that my machine was actually a 486DX. Apart from removing the case lid, and physically checking the CPU chip, is there any other way of telling whether or not I have been conned?
T.L. London

A   You shouldn't believe everything MSD (Microsoft System Diagnostics) tells you, especially if you're running it from a **DOS** window inside Windows 95. However, the more likely explanation is that your machine has a previously installed version of **DOS**, with an old MSD, that cannot recognise Pentium chips. Check the version number when the MSD intro screen appears – if it's earlier than v2.11 then that's the answer. Incidentally older versions of Windows 95 also have trouble identifying 'Pentium-class' processors made by AMD and Cyrix.

CHAPTER 4 **Printers and peripherals**

A printer and the other devices connected to your computer can extend its capabilities.

On its own a personal computer is not much use, unless you are content to just play games or gaze at whatever appears on the screen. In order to get a PC to do anything worthwhile it needs to be connected to external devices that make it possible for the machine to interact and communicate with the outside world. In the dreadful verbiage of the computer industry, these are known as 'peripherals'.

Most peripherals are linked to a Windows PC by parallel or serial 'ports'. A port is simply another name for a connector and parallel and serial refer to the way the port conveys data or information. Parallel connectors and cables generally have eight conductors, so eight bits of information can be sent simultaneously. A serial link uses a single line for data, and the bits travel, as it were, in single file.

Parallel connections are fast and some peripherals can be 'daisy-chained' together, to enable two devices to share a single port. However, cable length is limited to around three or four metres. Serial links are slower, but because there are fewer wires they are cheaper and more reliable, moreover they can operate over greater distances.

A PC can have up to three parallel ports (designated LPT 1 to LPT 3) and four serial ports (COM 1 through to COM 4), though most machines leave the factory with one parallel and two serial ports. Don't whatever you do shove the plug in any old port – you can easily bend the pins, and that could be expensive!

A printer is often the first and most useful peripheral you get – the chances are you may have got one when you bought your new PC. Printers fall into three basic categories: impact, laser and **inkjet**. Impact printers include **dot matrix** and **daisywheel** types but both are on the way out and really only suitable for plain text and simple graphics.

They are the Caxton presses of the computer world – you can still buy them, but they really are only suitable for specialised applications, like printing multi-part forms.

Laser printers are at the other end of the spectrum. They are appropriate for high demand business applications, where speed and quality are important. Prices are coming down, but some top-end models can still set you back several thousand pounds.

In the middle are **inkjet** printers, also knows as bubblejets, which are ideal for most home PC user and small office applications. They produce crisp-looking documents, sharp graphics, and most new models print in colour, in near photographic quality. They are slower than laser printers, but unless you are printing your thousand-page novel, they should be fine. Colour **inkjet** printers cost from as little as £100. There are many different models to choose from, so it's worth visiting your local PC store, to see and compare as many of them as possible.

Other devices that commonly use a parallel port connection are external disk and tape drives, and scanners. The majority of tape and disk drives are used for mass data storage, or backup, a subject we will be covering in greater detail in Chapter 6.

Scanners are like printers, but in reverse. They provide a means of getting text, graphics and images *into* a computer. Scanners can also turn your PC into a proper fax machine, scanning hand written documents and drawings, and turning them into fax files, that can be sent to other PCs, or ordinary office fax machines. We'll take a more detailed look at what they do and how they work in Chapter 12.

On many PCs the COM 1 serial port is used by the mouse, trackball or pointing device. COM 2 is normally the default port for an external **modem**; we will be taking a closer look at them in Chapter 9. (A lot of computers now come with an internal **modem**.)

In the past few years a variety of other devices have appeared that also require a serial connection. They include digital cameras (see Chapter 12), video and frame 'grabbers', radio tuners and camcorder edit controllers. Should you be some kind of gadget freak then most PCs can be fitted with extra ports, though it's normally easier to use an external switch-box – costing between £10 and £15 – so that a number of devices can share one port.

Printers in particular

PC printers bring to mind Dr Johnson's famous quip about performing dogs; the wonder is not that they do the job so well, but that they do it at all! The fact that these complex electromechanical devices are normally so reliable is another constant source of amazement. Until they go wrong that is...

In fairness, much of the time it's not the printer that is at fault but the software, and quite often it's due to incorrect installation of the **driver**. A printer **driver** is a small file that tells your PC everything it needs to know about how your particular printer works. Windows 95 comes with scores of **drivers** for popular makes and models of printer but it quickly becomes out of date as new models are developed, therefore it is always a good idea to use the **driver** that comes with your new printer, rather than the Windows offering. Take a few moments to check that you're using the right **driver**, particularly if your printer was bundled with the PC, and the **driver** was pre-installed.

Open My Computer and double click on the Printers icon. There you will see more icons representing all of the printer **drivers** your PC is currently using. There may be two or three listed, for faxing utilities etc., but one of them should be clearly labelled with the exact make and model number of your printer. If not, click on the Add New Printer icon to start the installation **wizard**. Make sure you have the **driver** floppy disk to hand and follow the instructions. Printer drivers can become corrupted so deleting and then re-installing the **driver** is always worth a try if you have begun to experience problems or unusual behaviour. Windows Help is also quite good at solving printer problems, always try that first (click on Help and key in 'Printer Problems'), before attempting any more complicated remedies.

If all appears to be well, highlight the printer icon by left clicking on it once, right click on the icon and scroll down the menu that appears. Select Properties. This will bring up a tabbed dialogue box, click on Details and once again check that the correct printer is listed. You should also see a button marked **Spool** Setting. Spooling is a technique that allows you to get on with some other task on your PC while the printer chunters away in the background. Printer files are shunted on to the hard disk, and sent to the printer when the PC's main processor has a spare moment – this happens so fast that it appears to be doing

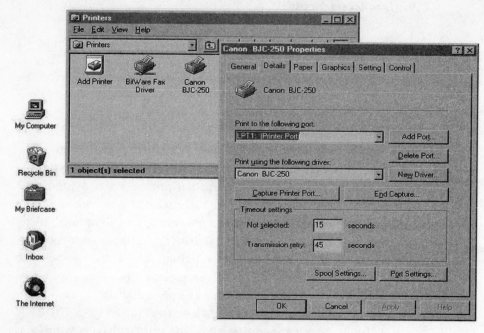

Printer Properties, make sure that the printer listed is the right model
and connected to the correct port

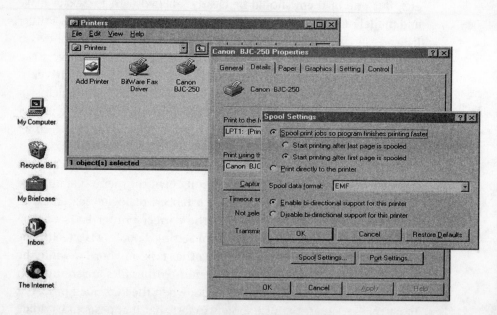

Problems with a printer could be connected with the Spool setting: only alter
one setting at a time, use the Restore Default button if you get in a tangle

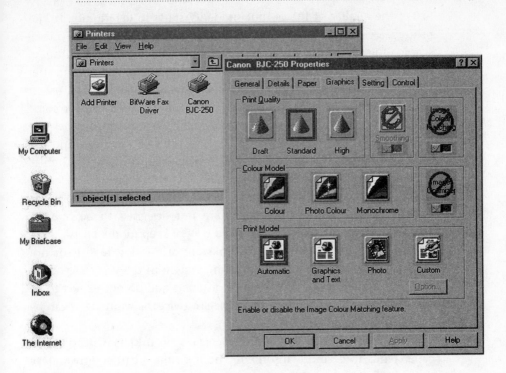

The Graphics tab on the Printer Properties window allows you to check
the colour settings

two jobs at once. However, spooling can sometimes cause difficulties
and if your printer is behaving erratically, or working very slowly, it's
worth changing the settings. Try altering the **Spool** Data Format from
EMF to RAW, or you could try the Print Directly to Printer option but
only change one parameter at a time and remember to change back to
the defaults (**Spool** print jobs) if it doesn't do the trick.

If your problems are concerned with the quality of the output, rather
than the operation of the printer, try changing the various performance settings that are available (depending on the make and model of
printer) on the Properties tabs. However, as the PC and printer between
them have probably adopted the factory defaults, more often than not
the problem, or problems, have something to do with the printer itself,
the paper, or the **consumables**.

Always keep new ink, toner or ribbon cartridges to hand and try that first if the quality of the output suddenly starts to deteriorate. **Inkjet** printers are usually the most troublesome in this respect as the microscopic holes in the printer head can become blocked, leading to partially formed characters, lines or streaking on images. If your printer has a self-cleaning routine (check the manual) you should use it regularly, particularly if the printer has been standing idle for some time, or you are about to print an important document on expensive high-grade paper. If that doesn't work, remove the cartridge and use the cleaning kit (if supplied) or gently wipe the head with a lightly moistened cotton bud. Don't try poking it with a pin or any other sharp object – you will destroy it!

Although most **inkjet** cartridges are not designed to be re-used, many types can be refilled. It's a good way of keeping the costs down, but bear in mind that some refill inks are of inferior quality, or not specifically formulated for the printing system in question. If you do use refill kits, only use good quality products and do not expect to be able to refill a cartridge more than once or twice. Be warned – it can be a very messy business!

Paper quality is very important, especially on **inkjets**. Cheap copier paper tends to be more absorbent; the ink runs – particularly watery cheap refill ink – and the characters become spidery and indistinct. Try experimenting with a variety of makes and grades of paper; special **inkjet** paper is usually worth the extra cost. Glossy paper, designed for use with colour **inkjet** printers can give excellent, near photographic results but it can be inordinately expensive, especially the small packets marketed by printer manufacturers. Try some of the cheaper brands that are coming on to the market, they cannot harm your printer – despite the dire warnings in some printer manuals – and some of them are very good indeed.

Keep the inside and outside of your printer clean. If there's a recommended cleaning and maintenance routine, stick to it. Always switch the printer off before you open up the cover. As with PCs it's better to blow than suck, so don't be tempted to shove a vacuum cleaner nozzle into the innards of your printer – use a can of compressed air or gas instead, and a new, clean paintbrush to remove stubborn debris. Finally, disconnect the cable to the PC and give the contacts a quick blow, wipe the casing over with a cloth dampened with water and a drop or two of washing-up liquid.

Q&A Solutions to real world problems

Paper waste

Q   My Canon printer often takes in two or more sheets of paper when printing. I use ordinary photocopier paper – is that okay, or should I use the more expensive **'inkjet'** type paper?
    F.D. Surbiton

A   Copier paper is fine. The trick is to 'fan' the paper before loading, this helps separate the sheets and dissipate any static charge that may have built up, which makes the sheets stick together.

Slow print

Q   Why does my printer run so slowly? I have a 233MHz Pentium PC and the printer is a recent Epson model. A page can take up to a minute to print, can that be right?
    D.F. via e-mail

A   No, that's far too long. A simple page of text shouldn't take more than ten to fifteen seconds to print. It sounds like you have the wrong **driver** installed, or it has become corrupted. Go to Printers (Start, then Settings), delete the existing **driver** and then go to Control Panel (Start, Settings), click on the Install New Hardware icon and follow the instructions to re-install the printer.

The family way

Q   I have just purchased a P200 multimedia PC for Christmas, with the intention that the whole family will use it. I will use it for accounts and letter writing, and the children aged nine and sixteen, want it for games and their schoolwork. I'll be waiting for the January sales, to get the best price but I have been given conflicting advice about which printer to buy. The shop where I bought the PC suggests a colour **inkjet**, but colleagues at work recommended buying a laser printer, the sort we use in the office, which gives superior results. Which type do you favour?

A.L. Surrey.

A   It's horses for courses. Laser printers are faster than **inkjets** and top models can produce crisper-looking documents, but **inkjet** printers are catching up fast. They're better for graphics and they're often a lot cheaper, both to buy, and to run. The performance of colour **inkjet** printers has improved enormously over the past couple of years and some models are capable of near photographic-quality results from digital still cameras – you might not own one now, but prices are dropping fast. Colour printers often come bundled with free software that can be used to create colourful greetings cards, invitations, banners and signs.

Print for posterity

Q   I have produced collections of local-interest photographs for the County Records Office and Libraries for over thirty years. As the photographs are for record purposes it is essential they will not fade. For this reason I have used monochrome, rather than colour photography, to take advantage of its superior light-fast properties. I now have a PC with a scanner and **desktop publishing** facilities. This ought to make my work much easier but I am concerned about the quality of the ink supplied for home printers. How permanent are they, compared with monochrome and colour photographic emulsions?

K.T. Leics

A   Your apparently simple question opened a real can of worms. The one thing we can say for certain is that nothing is permanent. According to Kodak, a photographic print processed in a professional laboratory and kept in ideal conditions, will last 'many decades'. Prints processed in high-street 'minilabs' are less durable and will deteriorate even faster if stored in PVC pouches or under PVC film in albums (PVC gives off chemically reactive fumes). Black and white images outlast colour ones by a significant degree.

PC printer inks also fade with time. A leading printer manufacturer claims the black inks used in consumer printers last for 'decades', provided the paper is stored in a dry and dark place. The best they could say for colour inks is that they will last for 'years' under the same conditions. Specially formulated UV resistant inks are also available for some printers, which will not fade for at least twenty years, when kept in a normal office filing system.

To make matters worse, a high proportion of the paper manufactured in the past fifty years – including that used for photographic prints – contains acids that slowly but surely cause it to self-destruct. Depending on how it's kept, this can happen in less than a hundred years.

Digital data, stored magnetically on disk and tape fares no better. There's evidence to suggest that magnetic recordings can survive for at least fifty years when stored properly. However, that assumes the equipment needed to replay or read the recordings is still available. Optical and magneto-optical storage media (CD-R/RW, **DVD-RAM**, MiniDisc) etc., should also be good for at least fifty years, but again, they are prey to format obsolescence. It seems the only way to guarantee longevity is to ensure your material is constantly copied!

Colour fast

Q   The price of colour printers seems to be falling rapidly – is there any new technology about to come on to the market that I should wait for, or is it safe to buy one now?
W.D. via fax

A   There's never a right time to buy a printer but that has nothing to do with new technologies, so you needn't worry about that (at least not for a while). Do your homework and buy your printer now. Shop around as there are some amazing deals to be had.

PCs in control?

Q   I've come across several references regarding the use of computers to control home appliances, but few hard facts. Can you tell me how easy, or difficult it would be to connect my computer to various devices, as I'm interested in the idea of home automation. What extra hardware and software do I need, and how much does it cost?
P.M. Winchester

A It can be done, but conventional home and office PCs do not have any facilities to control external equipment, other than standard computer peripherals. You will need a controller card. This fits into a spare expansion slot on almost any IBM compatible PC. It acts as an interface between the PC and the outside world, usually via a switch or relay board that can handle the higher voltages and currents needed to operate mains-powered devices.

There's virtually no limit to what can be done, with the right software. For example, you could use your PC to control central heating and security systems, switch lights on and off at preset times, even wake you in the morning with an alarm call and a cup of tea. PC control of systems and machinery is commonplace in the manufacturing industry, however, this is not an area the home PC market has been overly concerned with to date, so there are no simple off the shelf solutions. There are several useful books on the subject: *Micro Interfacing Circuits* by R.A. Penfold (Bernard Babari Books), and *Microcomputer Interfacing* by Joseph J. Carr (Prentice Hall International), are good places to start. They're both available from specialist bookshops, or Maplin Electronics, who also market a range of PC controller and switch boards, with software. Prices for controller boards start at around £80. Contact: Maplin Electronics 01702 554000.

CHAPTER 5 **Stepping on the gas**

It's time to pep up the performance of your PC
with some simple tweaks.

When your new Windows 95 PC left the factory it's highly unlikely
that it was set up for maximum speed and performance. Manufacturers
and vendors tend to be cautious and adopt the safest, most reliable
configuration. This is partly to stop you pestering their technical
support Helplines with problems that you'll be able to sort out
yourself, once you've gained a little experience; it's also quicker, and
cheaper for them to do it that way. However, it means that your
computer can probably be persuaded to perform certain tasks a little
bit faster, and speed up the action on some graphics-intensive games.

Before we get to the bits you can tweak yourself, it's worth pointing out
that the size of your PC's **RAM** has a big impact on how quickly it does
things. Windows 95 works best with 32Mb of **RAM**; if your machine has
less than that, have it upgraded. Memory chips are usually quite cheap
and it only takes a few minutes to install the new circuit boards.
Doubling your PC's **RAM** capacity from 16Mb to 32Mb, say, should cost
less than £40 and it can yield a speed increase of up to 50%. We're not
suggesting you do it yourself – though it's actually quite easy – but the
shop where you bought your PC should make only a nominal charge.
You will also then have someone to blame, if a problem should arise.

There are several things you can do to the Windows 95 **operating
system**, to pep up your PC, and they shouldn't get you into any
trouble, well, not much anyway. First make sure your hard disk drive
and CD-ROM are working at maximum efficiency. Right click on the
My Computer icon on the desktop, select Properties and then the
Performance tab. Hopefully you will see a message saying that your
machine is 'configured for optimal performance' but it's as well to
check. Click on the File System button and check the Hard Disk tab.

My Computer

Recycle Bin

My Briefcase

Inbox

The Internet

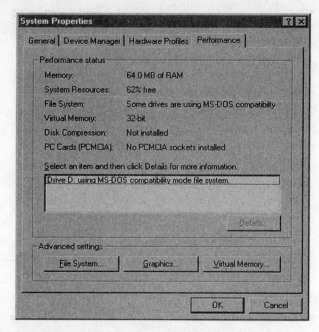

The Performance tab on System Properties gives you a general overview
of your PC's configuration

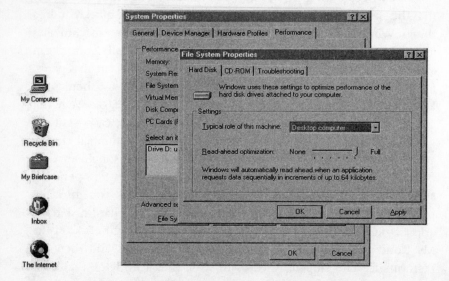

You can improve the performance of your CD-ROM drive by increasing
the Read Ahead Optimisation setting to 'Full'

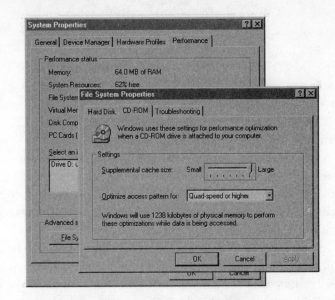

Make sure the File System Properties setting is correct for the CD-ROM
drive in your PC

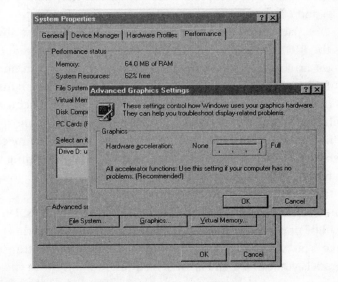

Changing the graphics accelerator setting can solve some types of
display problem

There you will see a window that outlines what sort of PC you have – make sure it is correct – and a slider that determines how the hard disk is used. If it's not already set to 'Full', change it.

Next click the CD-ROM tab, and set the 'supplemental **cache** size' slider to Large, assuming of course that the box below is correct and that your CD-ROM is a quad-speed model or higher. It almost certainly will be if your PC is less than a year or so old. Click on OK and you will return to the System Properties window.

Now click on the Graphics button. Ideally the Hardware Acceleration slider will be set to Full, if not, increase the speed, but be aware that this can cause problems on some systems. If you experience erratic behaviour, or programs freeze, move it back to an intermediate setting and see if that works.

As you begin to load more programs onto your PC, the hard disk drive will become cluttered with redundant files. These slow down how quickly information can be read from and to the hard disk drive. Removing those files will make the machine run faster and we'll be looking at how to do it in Chapter 10. You might be interested in some programs that will do the job for you quickly and safely, automatically optimising your PC. The best known are Quarterdeck CleanSweep, Cybermedia Uninstaller, Cross Atlantic Nuts and Bolts, and IMSI WinDelete. They mostly cost between £25 and £35 and it is money well spent.

One part of the PC set-up that manufacturers almost always ignore is the **BIOS** or Basic Input Output System. It's the program that runs as soon as your PC is switched on, telling it how to communicate with things like the hard disk drive – where all of your programs are stored – plus how much and what type of memory your machine has. It's a fair bet that some settings could be improved on most machines. Unfortunately the **BIOS** is off-limits to newcomers. In any case most of what you will see is incomprehensible, but there's nothing to stop you having a peek. As soon as you've switched on your PC you should see a message that says something like, 'to enter set-up press...'. It may be the 'Delete' button or some other combination of keys. Do it and you will be presented with a set of menus. Don't touch anything, but if you like, you can make a note of your PC's **BIOS** current settings – on some models you can use the Print Screen function on the keyboard. Keep it safe, you never know, it might come in handy one day. When you've finished choose the 'exit without making any changes' option.

Q&A Solutions to real world problems

Go-faster fonts?

Q   I have a self-built 486/66PC. It works wonderfully but seems rather slow, and I was wondering whether it has anything to do with the five hundred **fonts** my machine has stored? I daren't touch them because I read somewhere that terrible things might happen if I deleted any that were installed with Windows 95. I only use three families of **fonts** at the most, so what should I do?
M.M. via e-mail

A   The speed of your machine has little or nothing to do with the number of installed **fonts**. Most of the time they sit harmlessly in the background, minding their own business, so the only time you should consider removing any of them is if you need to free up disk space, and only then as a last resort. Leave well alone! There are plenty of other ways to make your PC run faster, but first check that the 'Turbo' mode hasn't been disabled on the **motherboard**. Remove all of the clutter such as unused files and programs from the hard disk, using a program like CleanSweep or Uninstaller, and run the Defrag utility, to speed up disk access. If you're using Windows 3.1, optimise memory usage with Memmaker. Finally, consider upgrading your machine. Increasing the size of the **RAM** is the simplest, cheapest and often the most effective method. Ultimately you could install a Pentium class CPU, or new Pentium **motherboard** and processor.

Out of time

Q   In common with most PCs my 486 DX2-66 has a time facility. I am most particular about clocks and watches being correctly set and am therefore surprised to find my PC 'losing' around 20 seconds per day. The firm who sold it to me told me this is well within tolerance. I find this amazing; my hundred-year-old grandfather clock is rarely out by more than 5 seconds a week!
J.P.F. Guildford

A   Errors of even a minute or more per day are not uncommon. There are basically two clocks inside an IBM compatible PC. General time-keeping is controlled by a battery-powered clock chip – similar to the ones used in digital watches – this lives on the **motherboard**. It runs all the time, even when the machine is switched off. Accuracy is generally quite good but they have to operate in a wide range of temperatures, so plus or minus a couple of seconds each day is about the best you can hope for. In any case it's only possible to set them to the nearest second.

The other type of clock, and the one that causes all the problems, exists in the PC's operating software. This only works when the computer is running. It sets itself to the hardware clock when the machine boots up, but thereafter relies on timing signals derived from a programmed interrupt in a **BIOS** subroutine. Depending on the PC's workload, and the type of software it's running, the timing signals can cause the clock to drift, gaining or losing time over the course of the day.

If you want a higher degree of accuracy – and this can be important in time-sensitive applications, where critical files or documents need to be precisely time-stamped – then you will have to install a second hardware clock in your machine, that gets its timing signals from an external source.

A program called Socketwatch automatically logs on to a selected master atomic clock whenever an Internet connection is made. It then automatically corrects the PC's clock. It is **shareware** and only works on Windows 95. It can be found at: http//www.midtenn.net/pub/mirrors/winsock-1/Windows95/time/

The bottom line is, if you want to know the time, it's probably not a good idea to ask a PC...

Sound barrier

Q   My CD-ROM drive won't play any of my music CDs through my PC's SoundBlaster audio system, however it will read normal CD-ROMs and the sound card plays sounds from other programs. Why?
M.L. via e-mail

A   In order to play audio CDs your CD-ROM drive needs to be connected to the sound card. The chances are either that yours isn't – it's not unknown for PC manufacturers to forget to fit the cable – or that it has become disconnected. Either way it's not difficult to fix. Disconnect your PC from the mains and remove the case lid. Don't forget to touch the metalwork to dissipate any static charge. The cable plugs into a small rectangular socket on the rear of the CD-ROM player; it can have 3, 4 or 5 pins. The cable is easy to identify; it's quite thin and round, coloured grey or black. The other end plugs into a similarly shaped socket on the sound card, which is in turn plugged into an expansion slot on the **motherboard**. The sound card is the one to which the speakers are connected. If there's no cable you will have to buy one. There are several different styles of plug and socket in use; rather than trying to remember the size or number of pins, get a universal audio cable that has all the common plug variants. They're available from PC dealers and mail order companies, like Choice, for around £6. Choice can be reached at: 0800 0730730.

Zip tip

Q   I have some .**zip** files stored on 3.5 inch disks – pictures downloaded from the Internet. How do I display or print them? When I try to open a file my computer activates an Acrobat Reader which responds with the error message that the file does not start with .pdf. Do I need to obtain a special reader program for these files, and if so where can it be obtained?
A.C. via e-mail

A   Files with the extension .**zip** are compressed, so they take up less room. To open, view or print the information, they have to be expanded or unzipped, using a file extraction program. The best known is a **shareware** utility called WinZip. It is very widely distributed on magazine cover disks and can be downloaded from numerous sites on the Internet, including the WinZip home page: http://www.winzip.com
    Once installed on your PC, WinZip will automatically open any zipped file, as soon as you click on it. You can view archived files, or extract them to the drive and directory of your choice.

Supply and demand

Q   I live on a fairly isolated stretch of the Dorset coast, and judging by the way the lights keep flickering, my house must be at the end of the electricity supply chain. It plays havoc with the TV, so what effect would it have on a computer?
J.G. Lyme Regis

A   Desktop PCs have fairly flexible mains power supplies, that can iron out small variations in mains voltage, though probably not the kind of instability you're suffering from. There's a very good chance you would end up with corrupted data, or worse. Your best option is to use a device called a UPS or uninterruptable power supply. They stabilise the supply, effectively isolating the computer from the mains. Even if the supply fails completely the UPS keeps the PC running on its internal re-chargeable battery, long enough for files to be safely saved. They're relatively inexpensive with prices starting at around £100 and they're widely available from computer hardware dealers. The other alternative is to use a laptop or portable PC, powered by its own battery pack. You could run it with the charger plugged into the power socket, to keep the battery topped up.

Need for speed

Q   My father has an unbadged 486 clone, possibly made by Mint, which he thinks has a 33MHz processor, 4Mb **RAM**, and a 210Mb HDD. At present he uses Windows 3.1, but the machine is slow, especially when he accesses the Internet. I want to upgrade his PC to Windows 95, which we both use at work, but I am unsure whether it is going to be economical. Is it worth changing, and if so, what size **SIMMs** should he purchase? If we do increase the **RAM**, will this speed the machine up?
P.M. via e-mail

A   First check the **modem**. If it is a 14.4kbps model, or slower, then this is the most likely cause of sluggish Internet performance. If that is the case, upgrading the PC won't make a blind bit of difference. In order to run Windows 95 the PC will need at least 8Mb of **RAM**, 16Mb would be better still. However, it is unlikely that it will operate any faster under the weight of Windows 95, it might even load and run some applications a lot slower. On the other hand, Windows 3.1 should fly along with 16Mb **RAM**.

Run off

Q   Most CD-ROMs supplied for a PC now state that they are Autoplay, and display the opening menu as soon as the disk is inserted into the drive. All was fine with my machine and this ran normally, but recently this function has not worked and I have to run programs the 'normal' way, i.e. using Windows Explorer or My Computer and clicking on the relevant program. Try as I might, I cannot get this function working again. References in Help only refer to Autoplay on audio CDs. Do you have any suggestions?
S.L. via e-mail

A   There are several possible causes; the most obvious being that the autorun function has become disabled. When a CD-ROM is loaded, Windows 95 periodically checks the disk directory for a file called Autorun.inf. (The flashing activity light on the front of the drive can become quite annoying, which is why a lot of people choose to switch it off.) If Autorun.inf is present on the disk, any programs listed in the file are automatically opened. To check or enable autorun, open Control Panel, click on the System icon then the Device Manager tab. You will see the CD-ROM drive listed; double click on it to reveal the **driver** then click on the open branch to show the Properties window. Select the Settings tab and use the mouse pointer to check the box marked Auto Insert Notification. You will then have to restart Windows 95 and hopefully all should be well.

CHAPTER 6 **Preserve your data from disaster**

If the worst should happen and all the priceless files on your hard disk are wiped, you'll wish you had arranged a proper backup system. Don't wait for disaster to strike, here's how to do it now.

How would you cope if the hard disk drive in your PC suffered a catastrophic failure or a virus scrambled all the data? A lot of PC owners gamble that it won't happen to them, but what if it does? Have you worked out how much you stand to lose? A faulty disk drive can be replaced, and you should have original copies of all the programs on your machine, but every letter, document, database or file you've ever created or downloaded from the Internet could be lost forever. If you use your PC for business, or to organise your personal finances or those of a club or society, the consequences could be very serious.

Thankfully hard disk crashes are quite rare these days and of course you take all sensible anti-virus precautions, don't you? Nevertheless, there's still plenty of other ways for data to be lost, from tinkering tots to power surges.

You know where this is leading – it's all about copying or backing up essential data, so that if the worst *should* happen, you can get your system up and running again. The trouble is that few PC users take the threat of disaster seriously, until it is too late.

It's not as though you have to buy a lot of expensive hardware; Windows 95 & 98 have a very capable backup utility built in. You can find it in My Computer. Simply right click on the C: drive icon, select Properties from the menu and then click on the Tools tab. Start the Backup **wizard** and follow the instructions; this will enable you to save your irreplaceable files to floppy disk. Backup compresses the data, thus saving space and it can be set to subsequently copy only those files that have changed. Backup can restore files just as easily, although obviously it only works when the system and Windows 95 are operating normally as shown by the illustrations below.

Half a dozen floppies should be enough to keep all of your important word processor and account files safe. However, this method quickly becomes tedious if you want to store more than a few megabytes of data. It's clearly impractical for large image files or applications, and no one in their right mind would contemplate using it to backup an entire system.

The alternative is a mass-storage device. Basically there are three types: magnetic disk, magnetic tape, and optical disk drives. Magnetic disks include high capacity floppies, and removable hard disk drives. There are a number of magnetic tape systems – sometimes called 'streamers' – using **QIC**, **DAT** and **8mm** data cartridges or cassettes. Optical disk storage covers recordable and re-writable **CD-ROM**, and the **DVD** format.

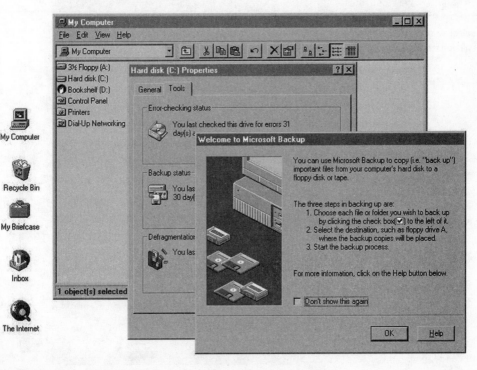

Microsoft Backup is built into Windows 95 and 98; it allows you to copy
all of your irreplaceable files to tape or disk

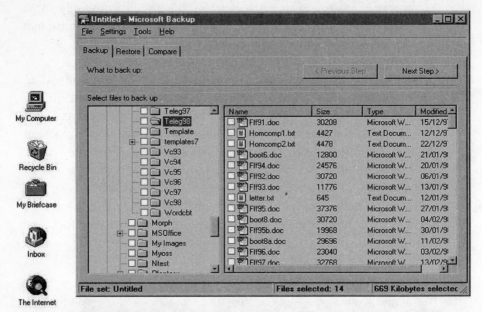

Select all of the files and programs you want to protect and Windows
will automatically back them up for you

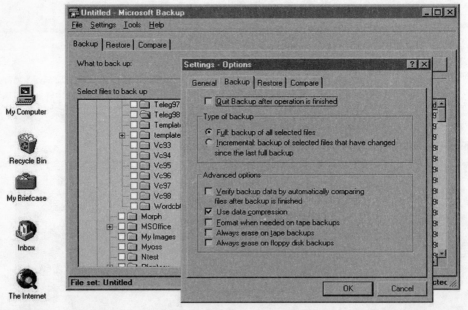

Backup can compress files to save space and selectively copy only files
that have been altered

High capacity magnetic disk drives are the simplest, cheapest and most flexible solution, suitable for the majority of PC users. They work in exactly the same way as a standard floppy drive, except that the disks – they look like fat floppies – have a capacity of between 100Mb and 2Gb (or up to twice as much when the data is compressed). Drives such as the Iomega Zip and Jaz or LS-120 drives from Panasonic and Imation fit inside the PC case. External models are also available; they communicate with the PC via an interface card, or use the parallel printer port. Most drives are quite easy to fit – external models are the easiest – and once installed, Windows 95 treats them as another disk drive, automatically assigning them a drive letter, usually E:. Files can be saved or copied to disk in exactly the same way as a normal floppy and as an added bonus they read and write data between five and twenty times faster.

The E: drive can be used in conjunction with Windows 95 Backup, or the utility programs supplied with it. LS-120 drives can also read and write data to standard 3.5-inch floppies and are normally configured to replace the A: drive. Prices start at around £85 for the Iomega Zip and Panasonic LS120 drives with a capacity of 100 and 120Mb per disk; blanks cost between £10 and £15 each. Jaz drives are available in 1 and 2Gb versions, costing £200 and £400 respectively, 1Gb cartridges are £65 each.

Removable hard disk drives are a good way of keeping a complete system backed up, though compared with high capacity floppies they're quite bulky and mechanically fragile. Prices have come down a lot recently; 2Gb models now sell for less than £200.

Magnetic tape drives, available as both internal and external types, can have an enormous capacity – up to 24Gb in the case of some professional devices, though most models can store between 2 and 4Gb of data. That means it is possible to copy the contents of an entire hard disk – including Windows 95 and all of your programs – on to one tape. The main disadvantage of tape is that it is quite slow; a 2Gb download can take two hours or more. That's not a problem for routine backups – it can be done whilst you're working – but if you just want to restore or update a single file it can take a long time for the tape to wind to the right spot. If the file size has changed, the whole tape may have to be re-written. Nevertheless, tape systems are reasonably inexpensive. For example, the Hewlett Packard Colorado 5Gb internal tape drive, with a capacity of 2.5Gb (5.2Gb when compressed) sells for less than £140 and tapes cost between £8 and £15, depending on the size.

Optical disk drives use recordable CD-ROMs with a capacity of up to 650Mb. CD recorders can read normal CD-ROMs and audio CDs as well, so they can replace the original drive fitted to your PC. There are two types of disk: CD-R disks can only be recorded once; CD-RW disks can be re-written, though you can't usually change files simply by writing over them, and so it may involve re-writing the whole disk. CD-R disks can be read on any CD-ROM drive, CD-RW disks require the drive to be 'MultiRead' compatible. Recordable CD drives such as the Mitsumi CR2600 cost from as little as £250. CD-R disks can be found for as little as £1 each, CD-RW blanks start at £17.

DVD drives are now reaching the shops, and recordable versions **(DVD-RAM)** have just begun to appear. **DVD** drives can play CD-ROMs and audio CDs but the important feature is disk capacity, which starts at 1.7Gb, though first generation drives are already up to 5.2Gb on double sided disks (2.6Gb per side). Further enhancements, including multi-layer disks will increase storage space to 17Gb, but that's still some way down the line. It's a little too early to talk about prices but it's likely they'll be comparable with recordable CDs within a year or two.

Most types of drive can be fitted in a few minutes, and they all come with relatively simple operating software and instructions. However, whatever system you use it's important to adopt a strategy or routine and stick to it. That means making regular backups. Most backup software can be programmed to complete the backup automatically, at a particular time. This doesn't have to interfere with your normal work as it can be done in the 'background' whilst you're engaged on another task – the computer makes use of the gaps and pauses that occur during normal operation.

If you are creating a lot of frequently changing files, it might be wise to back them up at least once or twice a day. It's no good keeping the tapes or disks in the machine; they must be stored separately. If your data is particularly vulnerable, you should think about making multiple copies, and keeping at least one of them off-site, in a secure location.

CONTACTS

Hewlett Packard, 0990 474747, www.hp.com

Imation, 01344 402000, www.imation.com

Iomega, 0800 973194, www.iomega.com

Mitsumi, 01276 290290, www.mitsumi.com

Panasonic, 0500 404041, www.panasonic.co.uk

Q&A Solutions to real world problems

Record keeping

Q   Can you tell me how long a backup copy, on a **zip** disk, is going to last? I bought my **zip** drive a little over eighteen months ago and two disks have already become unreadable.
A.D. via e-mail

A   In theory a magnetic recording – whether on tape or disk – should last for several decades, providing it is properly stored. It is possible that the disks you were using are faulty, but it is far more likely that they were kept close to a magnetic source, or in hot and/or humid conditions. Remember, a lot of electrical appliances give off strong magnetic fields, including PC monitors and speakers, telephones, fax machines and printers.

Missing copy

Q   I have an AST 812 computer, which I purchased new two years ago. It came pre-loaded with Windows 95. Recently I noticed that the Copy Disk command on the My Computer, drop-down File menu was no longer there. I can of course exit to **DOS** in order to copy a disk, but this takes a lot longer. Can you suggest why this command has disappeared, and a way of restoring it?
B.Y. Somerset

A Assuming that the Copy Disk option doesn't appear when you click the right mouse button on the floppy disk drive icon, the most likely cause is the Discopy.dll file is missing or corrupted. The solution is to restart the PC in MS-DOS mode and look for Discopy.dll in the Windows System folder. If it's there, rename it Discopy.old. Next, extract a copy of Discopy.dll from the Windows 95 CD-ROM (or Disk 11, in the case of Windows 95 on floppy disk) – it can be found in the Win95_10.cab cabinet file – copy it to the Windows System folder and type exit.

A pox on my PC

Q I run **Scandisk** and Defrag regularly on my PC but I have noticed that when doing a Defrag I get several clusters of tiny squares with a red mark in the upper right corner. The legend says that these are 'Data that cannot be moved'. The worrying thing is, they appear to be growing in number. It's a bit like the outset of measles. Why are they becoming more numerous? Can you suggest any way to get rid of them?

'Experts' have told me that it is a good thing to format the hard disk every six months. This seems a bit drastic, but I do have many spurious files scattered around my hard disk, which I would like to get rid of. I use CleanSweep regularly, but it is insufficient for my needs.

J.G. via e-mail

A Defrag identifies critical system files and data that, for one reason or another should stay put. The number of such files will increase as you add more software to your machine; even so they amount to no more than a very tiny fraction of your overall disk capacity, so it's nothing to worry about. Leave them alone and they won't bother you. There is no reason whatsoever to reformat your hard disk drive, unless it has become corrupted, or you have masochistic tendencies. CleanSweep is one of the most efficient uninstaller programs on the market. It is unlikely that any of the other packages will be able to identify any other redundant file groups more effectively.

Disk decisions

Q As a retirement project I am thinking of getting a computer with a view to storing and indexing the contents of a large number of photo albums. As this would entail large quantities of data, one of the new **DVD-RAM** drives, in conjunction with a PC and scanner, would seem to be suitable. However, this is likely to be a fairly expensive project, so any comments or recommendations would be welcome.
G.S. Berkshire

A **DVD-RAM** drives are coming down in price – the new Panasonic LF-D101 drive can be found selling for less than £400 – but you will probably find that recordable CD-ROM is a more cost-effective alternative. CD-ROMs have a 600Mb capacity, which means you can typically store between 500 and 1,000 **JPEG** compressed colour images on one disk. CD-ROM recorders can now be purchased for less than £150. Blank disks are cheap – from around £1.20 for write-once (CD-R) disks, to around £12 for rewritable (CD-RW) blanks. If you decide to upgrade at a later date you will still be able to read your CD-R/RW disks as all **DVD-RAM** drives will be backwards compatible.

Staying in contact

Q I have a large number of names and addresses in the Contacts section of Microsoft Outlook and would like to back these up for safety's sake. However, I have not yet found a way of transferring these files to a floppy. How can this be done?
J.D.A. via e-mail

A From the File menu select Import and Export to start the **wizard** helper program. Click on Export to a File option then Next, and from the list shown, choose Contacts. Click the Next button again and you will see a list of file types, select one from the list, click the Browse button and you will see the familiar file tree box, where you can choose floppy drive A: Click OK and it's done.

Lost address

Q   Is there a way of either printing out, or saving to a floppy my e-mail address book? I use Windows 95 and BT Internet and shortly after connection I had a major system crash which meant re-registering with my server and of course losing my address book which fortunately was not too long at that time. Now it is much larger and I am worried about losing it again so how can I back it up? I have laboriously typed it into a word processor file and saved on a floppy disk, just in case. The only non-manual way of preserving it that I have found so far is to send an e-mail to the entire list, including myself, and then printing out the return message – which annoyed a lot of people!
M.S. via e-mail

A   Your address book is contained in a file with the extension .wab and the particular one you are looking for is normally kept in the Windows 95 directory, though it may be buried in an application data folder. Either way, the easiest way to find it is to use the Find utility on the Start menu. Type in '*.wab' (without the quotation marks of course), and look for a wab file that starts with your user-name, or it may be called userMPS.wab. Note where it is located and send it straight to a floppy by highlighting the entry with the left mouse button, then clicking the right button. Click Send To from the menu and choose the floppy disk option. If you lose the BT Internet software again, after re-installation, you can restore the address book simply by copying your backup file back to the directory from whence it came.

CHAPTER 7   **Surviving a crash**

*The first thing you do when your PC stops
responding is panic. When that doesn't help,
try some of these suggestions...*

If Benjamin Franklin had been around today, it's a fair bet he
would have added Windows 95 crashes to death and taxes as another
one of life's certainties. It's not a case of *if* it is going to happen, but
when! Sooner or later, your PC is going to stop working, suddenly, and
without warning. It can happen while you're in the middle of
something, or it may simply refuse to boot up. Either way don't
panic. There is an almost infinite number of causes but in most cases
no permanent damage will have been done. If it happens when
you're working and you've followed our advice, you'll only lose a few
minutes' work, and hopefully have your PC up and running again in
no time.

Step one is to put some damage limitation measures into place.
If the software you're using has a facility to make automatic
backups, enable that facility and set a low delay time. Otherwise get
into the habit of saving your work to disk – hard and floppy – every
few minutes. It's worth investing in some crash protection software,
like Cybermedia First Aid 95. This program constantly monitors
your PC and the programs it is running. If it senses trouble, it steps
in and stops a full crash from occurring, and where possible,
suggests a remedy that will stop it happening again. Make sure you
have an up-to-date emergency start-up disk; if you don't, then make
one right away. Simply click on the Start button, then Settings,
Control Panel, Add/Remove Programs and the Start-up Disk tab,
then follow the on-screen instructions. (Full instructions are in
'Better late than never', in our collection of Windows 95 tips (see
Chapter 15.)

A program like First Aid could help you to survive a crash, and prevent it
from happening again

If a program freezes, the egg-timer won't go away or a blue warning
screen appears, whatever you do, *don't switch off*. This could cause even
more problems. Go and have a cup of tea as your PC may just have
gone into slow motion mode and might start responding again in a
few minutes. Well, it's possible, and it stops you doing anything hasty.
If it won't wake up try pressing the Ctrl, Alt and Delete keys, in that
order, just once, and you should see the Close Program window. Select
the offending programs from the list and click on End Task. With a
little luck it will close down – you can then safely close any other
programs that are running, and then shut down the PC or re-boot. If
that doesn't help then press Ctrl, Alt and Delete again to re-boot the
machine, and cross your fingers.

If the same program keeps crashing here's a couple of things to try.
From the Start button click on Settings, Control Panel and System.
Select the Performance tab and check the Graphics button. There

you'll find a slider for controlling graphics acceleration. Try the None, or Basic positions. Too high a setting is a common cause of lock-ups. Whilst you are in Control Panel click on the Display icon, then Settings and the Change Display Type button, and make sure the type of monitor shown is correct.

Software **drivers** that control the various items of hardware used by your PC, are a constant source of trouble, particularly following an upgrade. From the System icon in Control Panel click on the Device Manager tab and look for any black on yellow exclamation marks, next to the devices listed. If you spot any, fire up the Hardware Conflict Troubleshooter, which can be found in the Help menu; type Conflict in the Index field, double-click the highlighted selection and read the instructions.

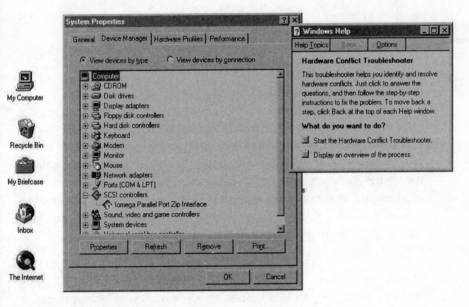

Windows Hardware Conflict Troubleshooter can help with many problems, simply type 'conflict' in the index field in Windows Help

When problems persist it's a good idea to start Windows 95 in Safe mode. This is a minimum configuration that bypasses potentially troublesome start-up files. Press F8 when the message 'Starting Windows 95' appears, after switch-on, and select option 2. If the PC appears to behave normally in Safe mode, repeat the procedure, this time choosing the Step by Step option, which hopefully will help isolate the problem.

If your PC and monitor powers up but won't boot, or Windows 95 refuses to load then dig out your emergency Start-up disk. It contains all the necessary files needed to get the PC going, at the very least into **DOS**, and hopefully, into Windows and Safe mode start-up. It contains several useful utilities to check and repair simple faults on the hard disk drive. There's also a program for editing the Windows 95 **Registry** files, which are behind a lot of crashes, but that's another, very long story...

Q&A   Solutions to real world problems

Lightning strikes again

Q   Here in Indonesia we are approaching the rainy season and the storms expected over the next few months will certainly be dramatic as usual. The lightning is impressive but there's usually little or no warning, hence my concern. My PC is connected to a US Robotics 56kbps **modem** and to simply unplug it is obviously the simplest solution, but so easy to forget. This would also leave me disconnected for much of the time. Surely there must be other alternatives?
R.R. via e-mail

A   The only sure way to protect your equipment from a direct lightning strike to power or telephone cables immediately outside your home or office, is disconnection. The electrical potential of a strike can rise to several tens of millions of volts, more than enough to arc over and fry any electronic component that gets in the way. However, there are several devices that can filter out high voltage spikes and surges, caused by the effects of an indirect or nearby strike. One of the leading companies in this area is Atlantic Scientific Corporation. ASC manufacture a wide range of surge protection devices, including stand-alone phone and mains filters. They also make a combined 'multimedia' model, with mains and phone surge protection, built into a single multi-way socket. This is marketed in the UK by Bowthorpe EMP, telephone 01273 692591; it sells for around £50. This model is fitted with UK 3-pin mains and BT phone sockets, which are obviously different to the ones that you are using. Details of surge protection devices designed for the Indonesian market, and local suppliers, can be obtained from ASC direct, via their well-maintained web site on: http://www.iu.net/atlsci/index.html

Millennium test

Q   Is there a sure-fire way to find out whether or not my computer is going to be affected by the so-called millennium bug? I have a PC with a Cyrix 200 MHz Pentium processor, bought in March 1997. Bear in mind I am nearly 70 and when I was receiving my formal education, the most powerful computer was 'Atlas' at Manchester University. *D.B. via e-mail*

A   There's a wealth of 'Y2K' test software on computer magazine cover disk and scattered around the Internet right now, but given the age of your machine, it is highly unlikely that you will experience any problems with the PC, or its **operating system**, following the year 2000 date change. There's an outside chance you may have to manually reset the date after 1 January 2000 – if your PC has an older **motherboard** and **BIOS** clock – and keep an eye on it on 29 February. Some PCs may fail to recognise the fact that the year 2000 is a leap year. Not all software is year 2000 compliant. Most programs written in the past two or three years – games, word processors, graphics packages – should work normally, but if you are using date-sensitive applications like financial software, payroll managers etc., then get in contact with the manufacturers for reassurance or an upgrade.

Power save

Q   My screen saver turns itself on after the set time. The problem is that

the screen goes blank after about 5 minutes. What is the reason for this and what can I do to rectify the problem?
D.L. via e-mail

A   It's not a problem as such. You are using an Energy Star compliant monitor and your computer is trying to cut your electricity bill, by turning off the monitor on the assumption that it is not being used. The timer control for the power save feature can be found by clicking on the Start button, then Settings and Control Panel. Double click on the Display icon and select the Screen Saver tab. Uncheck the Shut Off Monitor box, or increase the time setting.

Beligerent BIOS

Q   On turning on our 386 recently, our six-year-old accidentally typed in something during Start Up, so now we have a password-protected **BIOS**. Therefore we now cannot turn on the PC, or even boot it up from the FDD. Have you any advice on how to overcome this problem?
P.F. via e-mail

A   It should be possible to trick the **BIOS** into forgetting the password protection by removing the backup battery on the PC **motherboard**. This should return the **BIOS** to its factory default settings. However, this isn't a job you should tackle yourself and is best left to an engineer.

Stuck shut down

Q   I have upgraded from Windows 3.1 to Windows 95. When I shut down the computer it locks onto the 'Please wait until your computer shuts down' window. How do I fix this? I find Microsoft Internet support too tedious and unusable!
J.S. via e-mail

A   There's a very good chance this is due to a conflict between Windows 95 Advanced Power Management (APM) and the **BIOS** software on your PC's **motherboard**. When APM is enabled and you shut down the PC, Windows 95 sends what's known as a 'Set PowerState off' call to the system **BIOS**. The correct response is to switch the power off to the system, but if the **BIOS** doesn't recognise or support the call, Windows 95 will not shut down correctly and it usually stops responding. There are two possible solutions. The first is to switch off APM; you will find it in Control Panel. Double click on the Power icon and disable the Power Management setting. To solve the problem permanently, you will need to contact your PC supplier, and ask if there's a **BIOS** upgrade available.

Dead red

Q   I have a problem with my monitor, which occasionally loses the colour red. It seems to occur soon after booting up and after a while it rectifies itself, but it continues to lose colour sporadically.
M.G.J. Tyne and Wear

A   The fact that the missing colour returns when the machine warms up suggests a thermal fault, probably caused by an intermittent contact on one of the plugs or sockets that connect the PC to the monitor. This is one of the few places where red video information exists as a separate entity. It could also be the video card, not seated properly in its socket on the **motherboard**, or even a problem with the monitor itself. Check it out by substituting another monitor, or trying your monitor on another PC. If the monitor appears to be the problem, then try the monitor cable. Unplug it and squirt switch cleaner into the plug and socket contacts at both ends. If you're feeling bold you could also try re-seating the video card, though only do this if you're familiar with the innards of your machine. If that doesn't work the only solution is to have it checked by an engineer.

Hot and bothered

Q   My 133MHz PC has just begun to behave very strangely. The problem first started when I tried to print a document in Microsoft Word 6. The print-out was complete nonsense and when I tried again, the program froze. I re-booted the machine, but this time Windows 95 refused to load. Various error messages kept appearing and eventually, suspecting the worst, I tried to re-install Windows. This failed too. I gave up, but

when I tried half an hour later, the machine behaved completely normally. It has happened twice since then, usually after the machine has been on for a couple of hours. The problem usually disappears if it is switched off for an hour.
S.L. Sussex

A   The symptoms you describe are the sort of thing that can happen if the processor overheats. The usual cause is a failure of the on-chip fan. The blades can become clogged with dust, the motor or wiring can fail, or cables can interfere with the movement of the fan. A complete electrical failure is a possibility, although most fans are powered from the supply leads to one of the other disk drives. They're relatively cheap and easy to replace but if the fan appears to be functioning correctly, then it's a job for an engineer.

Don't knock it

Q   I own a Packard Bell 100MHz Pentium with 16Mb **RAM**. It is just over a year old but for the last three months it has crashed whenever it is slightly knocked, when a diskette is put in the A: drive, or even when there is a gust of wind! I was advised that it was a software problem but it has persisted despite reformatting the C: drive.
T.O. via e-mail

A   It has nothing to do with the software; there's an intermittent contact somewhere inside the case. You should have it checked by a qualified engineer but if you're handy with a screwdriver – and the warranty has expired – you might want to have a go at tracking it down. Disconnect the mains lead and remove the case lid. Touch the metalwork to disperse any static charge, then systematically remove and re-seat the cables and plug-in cards on the **motherboard** and disk drives. Only do one at a time and make sure you observe which way around they go. Don't unplug anything you can't easily get back in again.

Trip trap

Q   I recently purchased a new computer pre-loaded with Windows 95.

Everything was okay until I tripped over the power cord. Starved of power the computer shut down. Now when I start it up, the blue Windows screen appears and it goes into **DOS**. I tried typing 'win' to get back to Windows 95 but the computer just repeated the start-up procedure, then went into **DOS** again. This time I tried 'exit' but to no avail. How can I get back into Windows?

A.C. via e-mail

A   A sudden power interruption will normally only result in the loss of whatever it was you were working on at the time. However, problems can occur if it happens when the machine is writing or updating critical files on the hard disk. It's impossible to say which ones will have been affected, or how much damage has been done, but you might be able to isolate the problem by starting Windows 95 in 'Safe' mode, which bypasses the main start-up files. During the boot-up sequence, when it reaches 'Starting Windows 95', press the F8 key. Select option 2, to see if Windows will load in Safe mode. If so, exit Window, re-boot the machine and select option 5, 'step by step confirmation' and follow the on-screen prompts to the point at which the machine stumbles. You could also try the 'Logged (\BOOTLOG.TXT)' option, which creates a log of the boot-up sequence that will be filed in the C: root directory. It will probably contain a number of error statements, but the one you're interested in will be the last entry.

The long goodbye

Q   My Windows 95 machine is taking longer and longer to shut down. Sometimes it hasn't shut down five minutes after clicking Shut Down on the Start menu and occasionally it will not shut down at all. Any help would be appreciated.

C.C. via e-mail

A   This is a very common problem and there are many possible causes – here are just a few of them. A corrupt Close Program or Exit Windows sound file could be causing the system to hang. Check they're okay, or cancel them from the Sounds utility in Control Panel. Make sure that no programs are left running in the background when you shut down. Press Alt-Tab and check the task menu is clear. If that's inconclusive, press Ctrl-Alt-Delete to call up the Close Program menu. Highlight each selection and Click on the End Task button, to find out if any of the programs listed – except Explorer – have stopped responding. You might come across applications loaded automatically by Windows at start up; one of these could be causing problems. If it's the same one each time, then that's your culprit. If that doesn't help, there's probably something amiss in one of the start-up files (e.g. autoexec.bat, win.ini or config.sys) or the dreaded Windows **Registry**, and that will require further, much more detailed investigation.

Moaning mini

Q My PC mini tower case has recently taken to emitting a dreadful moaning sound on start up – something between a baleful dirge and a cow in pain. My system is fairly new and the manufacturers assure me there's nothing to worry about. They say part of the workings may have dropped out of place – possibly the fan – and it will grind itself down shortly, after which the problem will go away. I wondered if you had ever come across anything like this before, and if so, have you any advice, apart from returning the machine?
J.W. North Yorks

A Nine times out of ten, bovine-like moaning sounds come from the CPU cooling fan. Sometimes a dry bearing causes it – some of those fans are very cheap and nasty – or it could be a cable rubbing against the blades. Either way it needs attention. Waiting for it to grind itself down is definitely not a good idea! If the PC is still under warranty the vendor is obliged to put it right, although if it is an obstructed fan, you might want to fix it yourself, rather than suffer the nuisance of sending the machine back, or waiting for a visit from a service engineer. To do so, unplug the machine from the mains and remove the case lid. Make sure you earth yourself on the case before touching anything. Locate the fan, which should be clipped to the processor chip, on the **motherboard**. If there are any cables fouling the fan blades, gently move them out of the way. If the fan is clear and the noise persists, then it's going to have to be looked at.

Fatal distraction

Q   I have a Packard Bell 909D with 8Mb of **RAM**, an 850Mb hard disk drive, plus Windows 95 and various programs installed by the manufacturer. I have experienced a number of recurring problems, with error messages like 'A Fatal Exception' or 'A Fatal Error has occurred' and the computer occasionally freezes when I close down. What do they mean?
K.M. Southampton

A   There's a good chance that at least some of the error messages are due to your PC's lack of memory. You should consider upgrading your computer's **RAM** to at least 16Mb, and preferably 32Mb. Windows 95 will just about run on a PC with 8Mb of **RAM**, but it's not happy...

CHAPTER 8

Virus protection

The risk of your PC picking up an infection is small, but real. Here's a few ways to protect your system.

Friday the 13th occurs at least once or twice most years and it's a worrying date for superstitious PC owners. It's a favourite time for triggering computer viruses, but relax – the chances of your PC catching a nasty infection are actually quite small, provided you take a few simple precautions.

Nevertheless, the risk exists and with the growth of the PC population, the Internet and the ingenuity of virus creators, it is increasing all the time. But what exactly is a computer virus, and what are the dangers to your PC?

Broadly speaking, a virus is any program that gets into your PC, without your permission, and interferes with its normal operation. At the last count there were more than 15,000 of them. As it happens, most are relatively benign and do little actual harm, apart from messing around with the display or putting up irritating messages on the monitor screen. Others though can do real damage, to the data on your PC or the network, by scrambling or concealing files and causing unpredictable behaviour. In extreme cases a virus can trash the hard disk in your computer, where all of your programs and files are stored.

Viruses come in all shapes and sizes but they've all got individual characteristics or 'signatures', which can be identified by up-to-date anti-virus scanning software. Some of the hardest to detect lurk in the Master Boot Sector, which is an area of your hard disk that contains important software, which controls how your PC operates. From there, viruses can spread to floppy disks and thus infect other machines.

Almost as virulent are memory resident, or **TSR** file viruses, which can also take over a PC's **operating system** and make it do unpleasant things to files and data. They live quietly in the computer's memory and spread by infecting files containing programs and **drivers**. They're the ones that end in the letters .exe, .com or .sys.

Stealth and polymorphic viruses are cunning little devils. They're a bit like their biological counterparts. They can change their appearance and incorporate themselves into legitimate pieces of software, making detection and eradication that much more difficult. Some hide by making sure that the size of the host program doesn't change after it has been infected. Others alter their signature code after each infection, to avoid being identified by scanning software.

Macro viruses are comparatively new and a threat to PCs running word-processing and spreadsheet programs. They're written in a programming language that makes the program perform a repetitive task or 'macro'. The trouble is, macros can be hidden inside text and data files and easily transferred from PC to PC via infected disks and e-mail. Once the file is opened the virus goes about its business, changing and corrupting other files.

Incidentally, your PC cannot become infected by plain text e-mails. Viruses have to be hidden inside attachments and programs, and they only become active when they're opened or executed. It's fair to say that the Internet is generally safe, though it's sensible to avoid downloading material from obscure or suspicious-looking sites.

If your PC is mostly used for game playing or word-processing then you haven't much to worry about. The odds start to rise when your machine is connected to the Internet or a network, or when you swap disks with other PC owners or buy bootleg and pirate software. The odd virus has also popped up on free magazine cover-mounted CD-ROMs. If your PC use falls into any of these categories, or if you have already experienced an infection or your machine is behaving erratically, then it's time to get hold of some anti-virus software.

Most anti-virus programs carry out a preliminary scan as they're loading, so you start with a clean slate. After that they check vulnerable areas of your disk drive and memory, every time the PC is switched on. All new software coming onto the machine is checked, whether it's on disk, CD-ROM or downloaded from the Internet.

Anti-virus software is only as good as its signature library. This is a collection of identifiable virus codes and behaviour patterns that instruct the PC to carry out a damaging operation, therefore, providing the code or pattern is in the library, the software can recognise and deal with that virus. Most programs can be updated, with signatures of the newest viruses, either automatically from the manufacturer's Internet web site, or on floppy disk.

If an infection is detected, scanning software immediately puts up a warning message on the screen, and stops any further potentially damaging disk writing activities. The affected files are then isolated or 'quarantined', so they can be safely disinfected, deleted or renamed, if the software regards them as harmless. Don't get paranoid but do take precautions!

Which virus?

The cost of anti-virus software reflects the speed of operation, manufacturer's backup, and to a lesser extent, the depth of protection. They are important considerations on multi-user business systems and networks. However, for most desktop PC users, general-purpose packages like Norton AntiVirus and McAfee VirusScan are more than adequate. PC-cillin is very well presented, and particularly well suited to newcomers.

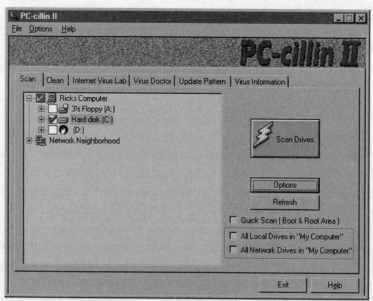

An antivirus program like PC-cillin II automatically carries out a virus sweep every time the PC is switched on

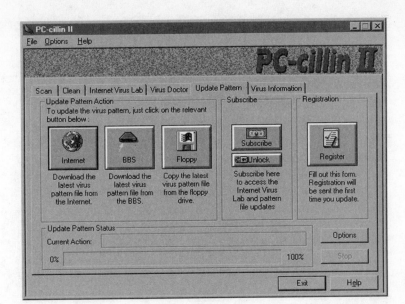

Most virus checkers have the facility to update their signature library by
downloading files from the Internet

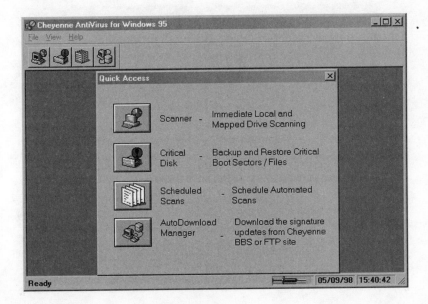

A good virus checker has plenty of options that will allow it to
constantly monitor your PC

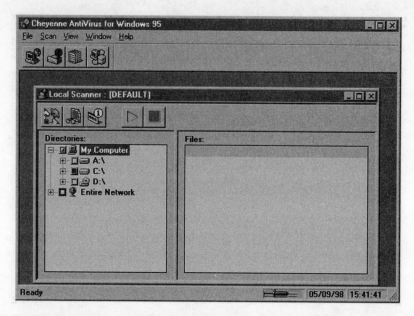

A clean bill of health, this time, but viruses are a constant threat

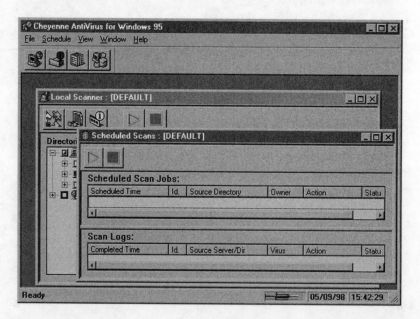

It's a good idea to schedule a virus checker to carry out its checks at a
particular time, in case you forget

Anti virus software

Cheyenne Anti Virus
Roderick Manhattan Group Ltd., tel. 0181 875 4441
http://www.cheyenne.com

Dr Solomon's Anti Virus Toolkit, Win 95
Dr Solomon UK, tel. 01296 318700
http://www.drsolomon.com

McAfee VirusScan V3
McAfee, tel. 01344 304730
http://www.mcafee.com

Norton AntiVirus Deluxe 4.0
Symantec UK, tel. 0171 616 5600
http://www.symantec.com

PC-cillin 95
Roderick Manhattan Group Ltd., tel. 0181 875 4441
htt://www.checkit.com

Sophos Anti-Virus 3.0
Sophos plc, tel. 01235 559933
http://www.sophos.com

Q&A Solutions to real world problems

Beat the bug

Q   My PC has begun acting strangely – it crashes frequently and sometimes it won't switch off. Could a virus have caused this? It started
happening a few days after I signed up for an Internet connection.
K.L. via e-mail

A   It is unlikely, as viruses do not tend to make PCs unreliable. Your machine is almost certainly suffering from good old Windows 95 instability, and the cause is more likely to be a corrupted program. Try to establish when and how the problem occurs and this should help you, or an engineer, pinpoint the fault.

Cover up

Q   Could a virus get into my PC from a free CD-ROM on a computer magazine? I have seen several that I would like to try, but I'm reluctant to risk my normally reliable machine.
H.J. Chichester

A   It can and has happened, but most magazines go to great lengths to ensure their disks are virus-free. If you're in any doubt, run the programs through a virus checker first.

First aid

Q   What should I do if I suspect a virus is infecting my PC? Will switching it off make any difference?
K.D. Exeter

A   It may not be immediately obvious that a virus is at work, and it's not easy to distinguish between normal activity and a virus doing its dirty work. However, if after opening a program you see any unexpected messages or threats, switch the PC off straight away and this might limit the damage. Nevertheless, the safest solution is to install some virus protection software; this will constantly monitor your PC, looking out for any suspicious actions, such as deleting or overwriting critical system files.

Virus protection

Q   I am a very late starter with computers but am enjoying every minute; however, whenever I download files from the Internet I always get the warning that these files could contain viruses. This leads me into the dilemma of whether to continue or not. How can I protect my system from something unknown? I have taken the chance on occasions and sometimes it has been worthwhile, but on others the script has been complete scribble and I haven't been able to read it anyway. Any help would be appreciated.

P.A. via e-mail

A   The virus warning is automatic and if you read on, it suggests that the file should be saved to disk where it can do no harm. If there is a virus in the file it will only be activated when the file is opened or un-compressed. The solution is to install an anti-virus program on your machine, so that once the file has been downloaded, it can be checked for infection. Once it's given the all clear it can be safely opened.

The downloads that contained gobbledegook text were probably encoded binary files, which cannot be read or viewed until they have been extracted, using a small utility called uudecode. Unfortunately it's not that easy to use but there is a **freeware** program called uudeview, which is much more user-friendly. It's self-extracting, so once it has been downloaded (and virus checked), just click on it, and it will auto-matically install itself on your PC. You can find it, along with a useful introduction to this kind of file coding at: http://www.unifrankfurt.de/%7Efp/uudeview

Boot sale bargain?

Q   I bought a second-hand hard disk drive at a car boot sale recently. I connected it to my PC and configured it as the slave to drive C:. Almost as soon as I changed the drive directory to see what was on it, the PC started behaving oddly, writing a huge number of files to the C: drive, which I have been unable to access. The PC still works normally, and I am able to use the new drive, but I'm worried that the mystery files may be a hidden virus.

G.P. via fax

A   It's possible, though a little unlikely that this is the action of a virus. Buying second-hand PC components is a risky business and you should have taken precautions. At the very least you should have formatted the drive as soon as it was installed. You should now install a virus checker program to scan your system, and format the new drive, before it causes any damage.

Lock out

Q   I am trying to prevent people from logging on to my home computer without a password, possibly infecting my machine with programs containing viruses. I have tried to use the Windows 95 Logon window, but there are two ways to bypass this; either by pressing cancel or by putting in a new user name and password, which the computer accepts. Is there any way of only allowing users on the computer whose password/username I have approved?
T.W. via e-mail

A   You're right, Windows 95 is not very well protected but there are several powerful security programs on the market that can prevent your PC from being used without your consent. Unfortunately they tend to be quite expensive – typically £50 to £70 – so it's worth looking at what the **shareware** market has to offer. Workstation Lock from Posum Software will do everything you require. If you end up using the program it is good manners to send the author a licence payment, in this case a very reasonable $5.00. The file download can be found at: http://posum.com

Taking the biscuit

Q   On the Internet, I frequently get a message to say I have a 'cookie' followed by a file number. I am then asked if I want to accept it. There is a threat that the page I am downloading will not be complete if I say no. What are **cookies**, are they dangerous, could they contain viruses and should I accept them or not?
T.H. via e-mail

A   **Cookies** are generally harmless and pose no threat from viruses. They're small packets of data, kept by your Internet **browser** software and stored on your hard disk; you should find them filed under 'cookies' inside your Windows directory. They're created and used by the web server computers you access, to help them configure the way web pages are presented on your PC. They also speed up access and file transfers.

Whenever you select or key in a web site address your **browser** first checks to see if you've been there before. If you have, there may be a cookie, which it sends, along with the request for the web page, so the web server doesn't have to waste time finding out what software you're using. **Cookies** can contain a variety of information, including whether your **browser** can display frames, or just text. If the site has restricted access the cookie will include your password, PIN or account number or a range of personal preferences. This information will only be passed on to the specific web site that compiled the cookie in the first place. They cannot be used to divulge your e-mail address, unless you have already provided it, by filling in a form, when you previously used that web site.

Portable plague

Q   I am thinking about buying a palm-top PC, probably one of the Windows CE models, though I haven't entirely ruled out the Psion 5. Are you aware of any viruses that can affect these machines, and is there any anti-virus software available?
D.D. Greenwich

A   So far palmtops seem to have been spared and as far as we're aware there is little or no risk of infection to either Windows CD or Psion machines.

CHAPTER 9 **Going online and the Internet**

For many, the lure of the Internet is one of the main reasons for having a computer, but if you're still not convinced, here's a few more reasons to get connected.

If you've never used the Internet, you're probably wondering what all the fuss is about. So what is it, and what can it do for you? The first bit is easy; the Internet is a world wide network of computers – millions of them, from small desktop machines to huge industrial mainframes – all talking to one another using a common language and address system called TCP/IP, the computer equivalent of Esperanto. Yes, more technical mumbo-jumbo but fortunately you don't have know what it means. (In case you're wondering though, it stands for Transmission Control Protocol/Internet Protocol.)

The second question is harder to answer. The Internet is as diverse as the millions of people around the world who use it. For example, train-spotters, stamp collectors or any special interest group for that matter, use it to share news and gossip, and keep in touch with other like-minded enthusiasts. For academics and researchers it is a way to access and disseminate information. It's a fast, cheap and efficient means of sending and receiving text messages, otherwise known as electronic mail or e-mail. The point is, whatever your proclivities – however mundane, obscure or just plain weird – you will find them catered for on the Internet.

In order for your PC to connect to the Internet, send and receive e-mail or faxes, or communicate with other computers via telephone, it needs a device called a **modem. Modem** is computer jargonese for MODulator-DEModulator; it's a typically obscure way of saying that it converts digital data into audible tones (and back again) that can be squirted down an ordinary telephone line. They're the squeaks and bleeps you hear when you dial up an Internet connection.

A word of warning – **modem** technology is completely out of hand! It is responsible for more baffling TLAs (three letter acronyms) than almost any other area of computing. Don't bother trying to understand what they all mean, it's simply not necessary in order to use one and life's just too short.

It does pay to learn one or two terms though, so you can appear knowledgeable to PC salespeople, and not get ripped off. There are basically three types of **modem**. Internal modems are plug-in **expansion cards** that live inside your PC. External modems are small boxes with lots of winking lights that connect to a socket or serial 'com port' (see Chapter 2) on the back of your PC. **PC card** modems are the smallest; they're like thick credit cards and they fit into a slot on the side of laptop computers.

Modems can be further sub-divided into data-only and voice-data types. The former is used for general purpose Internet access and faxing while voice **modems** can process speech as well, and come with extra software that can turn a PC into a sophisticated telephone answering machine.

The next most important thing to know is that **modems** operate at different speeds in terms of how quickly they can send and receive data. The simple rule of thumb is the faster, the better. **Modem** performance can be measured in a number of ways but the figures you'll see quoted most often on PC specifications and adverts, are bits per second or 'bps'. The current norm is 33,600bps, usually abbreviated to 33.6kbps; it's really not worth bothering with slower **modems**, unless you're very patient, and a BT shareholder.

In theory 33.6kbps is the fastest speed possible on the public telephone network, or at least down the wires and cables that link your home to the telephone exchange. After that, connections between exchanges and the network of computers that make up the Internet, are via high-speed digital lines. That means data can be sent back to your PC faster than it can send it, which has allowed **modem** designers to increase speeds to 56kbps. However, this trick only works one way, from the Internet to your PC as the computer can only send data at a maximum of 33.6kbps. The only difficulty with 56kbps modems is that there are two competing standards. A resolution is expected shortly and pretty well all 56kbps **modems** should be able to have their **operating software** upgraded. In any event all 56kbps **modems** will function at 33.6kbps.

It is possible for your PC to communicate at even higher speeds, if you're willing to shell out for a digital telephone line or ISDN (integrated services digital network). Speeds of 64kbps and more are possible but it is expensive, both for the initial connection, and then line rental. ISDN **modems** are a lot dearer too. BT is currently reviewing their charges, but it is likely that ISDN will only make sense for businesses for some time to come.

Setting up a **modem** on a PC used to be a nightmare, but Windows 95 has made it a lot easier. Most new modems are designed to 'plug-and-play'. Once connected, they are automatically configured using the add/remove hardware utility in the Control Panel. This is accessed from the Start menu under Settings; simply click on the icon and follow the instructions.

Setting up an Internet account is also very easy. The installation disk (CD-ROM or floppy) normally supplied free by the Internet service provider or ISP will take you through the procedure step by step, identifying and testing your PC and **modem** as it goes. You will be asked to enter your name and address, and then it will call up the ISP's server computer. Remember to have your credit card handy as you will have to enter the number, which will result in your being issued with an ID number and/or e-mail address, or you can choose one for yourself, provided no one else is using it. If everything goes smoothly you can be surfing the net in about ten minutes.

We're not going to get into the debate of which ISP has the fastest connections or offers the best value for money; the truth is that the market has become fiercely competitive and they're all much of a muchness these days. Charges vary but with moderate use it typically works out at less than £10 a month. That doesn't include the cost of phone calls while you are 'on-line', these are normally charged at BT's local call rate, costing from as little as 1 pence per minute at weekends.

Ask friends and colleagues for recommendations, and heed their warnings. Most companies offer free trials, so you can play the field. One word of caution though, Internet software is not very sociable. If you have more than one Internet access program on your PC – from a free cover-mounted CD-ROM say, they can clash and make your PC behave erratically, so make sure you completely remove any other Internet programs from your PC, before you install a new one.

Internet access opens up numerous possibilities in addition to browsing the World Wide Web and using e-mail. Internet telephony is one of the most interesting, especially if you have friends or family living abroad. It only works PC to PC, and both parties have to be on-line at the same time, but you can hold a fairly normal two-way conversation with someone on the other side of the world, for the cost of a local call. It's possible to see them as well, with an Internet video-phone link, though it might be a good idea to wait a while, as there's still a lot of confusion over technical standards.

On the net

If you have got your Internet account up and running let's look at how to get the most out of your e-mails, and begin exploring the Web. But first a short history lesson. The Internet began 30 years ago, as the Advanced Research Project Agency Network (ARPANET); a US Department of Defense-funded program, providing a secure and survivable communications medium for organisations involved in the American defence industry. The Internet as we know it today was created in 1983, as a civilian spin-off from ARPANET, called NSFNET (National Science Foundation Network), used by commercial enter-prises and educational establishments. However, it didn't really take off until the early 1990s when home PCs became affordable, and following the development of the World Wide Web.

Essentially the Web is a set of software standards, used to create a simple graphical interface, similar in some respects to Windows. In other words it is highly visual in nature and you make things happen by moving a mouse pointer and clicking on icons, buttons, pictures or highlighted text that appear on your computer screen. Because it's so easy to use, the World Wide Web has become the single most important component of the Internet, closely followed by e-mail. It's also worth knowing that the Internet is widely used to move files from one computer to another, with a procedure called FTP (file transfer protocol), and to remotely access distant computers using a system known as Telnet.

Don't worry about the jargon, all you need to join in the fun is a PC, a **modem** and an Internet account. Almost any type of PC will do, from a humble Sinclair Spectrum, to a top-of-the-line IBM PC compatible or Apple Macintosh, though up-to-date machines make it a lot easier. More recently we've seen the arrival of set-top Net TV boxes, that hide all the computer gubbins in a black box, connected to an ordinary television receiver.

So now you've loaded the free trial software, or signed up for Internet access through Windows 95, given a complete stranger the right to dip into your credit card account and in return you've been given a password and e-mail address. You're ready to start surfing, but hold on a minute – there's a few things you should do first.

Get to know your **browser**. That's net-speak for the software program that gives you access to the Internet. A browser's job is to search out information and present it on your screen, in an easily digestible format, using the same familiar conventions and mouse-clicking operations that you use in most other Windows programs. There are several different **browsers** in use at the moment but the chances are, you'll be using Microsoft Internet Explorer, Netscape Navigator, or a customised version based on one of them, supplied by one of the major Internet service providers (ISPs), such as BT Internet CompuServe or AOL. The presentation varies but they all do the same basic job, and certain features are common to all types.

You don't have to commit to a particular **browser**; once you have an Internet account, you can change at any time. Microsoft Internet Explorer is still included as an integral part of Windows 95 – despite a US court case – and Netscape Navigator is often bundled with new PCs as well, and is widely distributed on computer magazine cover disks, or included with CD-ROMs. Simply load the new **browser** and enter your e-mail address and you can use it straight away; Windows 95 will automatically enable it for use with your **modem** and Internet connection. Likewise, you don't have to stick to the e-mail address issued by your ISP. You can find out how to change it in the associated Help file or on the service provider's home page. However, it's unlikely your first, second or even third choice will still be available, unless you have a really unusual name.

If you want to visit an Internet site straight away, and you have the address in front of you, click on your **browser's** 'Go' or 'Open' button, or type the address into the empty field on the browser's tool bar. Otherwise a window with a blank field will open. Make sure every dot, slash and colon is correct and in the right place, for the Internet is incredibly pedantic. Click OK and your **modem** will start dialling. Within a few seconds you should hear a burst of bleeps and squeaks, which tells you the connection has been made and your PC is talking to your ISP's server computer.

What happens next, depends on the speed of your **modem**, the time of day, the quality of the line and the content of the page you're downloading. Hopefully you will see a fully formed page within a few seconds but it can take a minute or more to load, if there's a lot of complex graphics or images. Things slow down dramatically in the early afternoon, when east-coast America wakes up and starts surfing. Switching off the graphics – an option in the Preferences menu of most

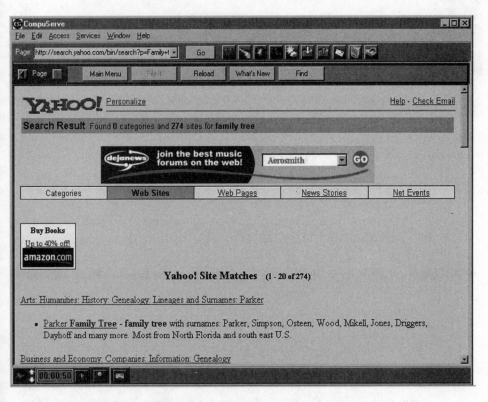

A search engine like Yahoo! can help you find what you're looking for, in this case a name search, to help compile a family tree

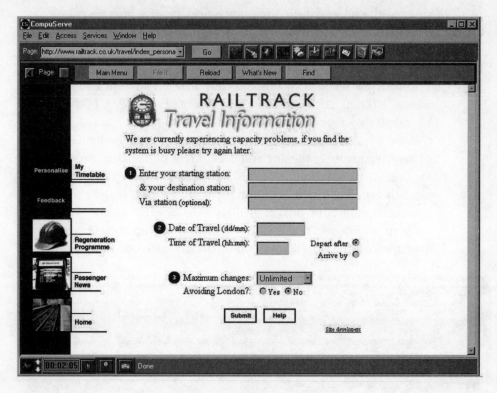

Planning a trip? The Internet can help you with timetables, route
planners and essential, up to date information

browses – can help speed up the display, particularly if the information you're after is mainly text.

If there's a particular subject, topic or products you want information on, but don't know where to look, use one of the many **search
engines** on the Internet. These are Internet sites that work like automated directory enquiries, and they're free to use. They can sift
through millions of documents and web sites in a matter of seconds,
using a few key words or short phrases.

A good place to start is the Web's most popular and comprehensive
search engines, Yahoo and Lycos; they can be found at www.yahoo.com
and www.lycos.com respectively. As soon as the opening search page
appears, click the 'bookmark' or 'add to favourite places' button on your
browser. Get into the habit of using this facility as it saves a lot of time.
Try to be as specific as possible when you type in search keywords,

If you play computer games the Internet is essential; web sites like this
one can supply you with the latest hints and cheats

otherwise you'll be swamped with hundreds or even thousands of 'hits',
most of them irrelevant.

Sending and receiving e-mail is easy. You will be told if there are any
messages waiting for you every time you log on. You can read them
straight away, though it's quicker to download them into your PC, so
you can read them at your leisure. Your **browser's** message or mail
window is fine for composing and sending a few lines of e-mail, but
they're a bit cramped. If you want to send more than say, a hundred
words, it's far easier to use a word processor. First, write your copy in
the usual way on the word processor page then highlight all of the
text, normally by clicking into an empty area of the screen, to the left
of the first word and dragging the mouse pointer to the end. On some
word processors you can also highlight a whole document by clicking
the left mouse button three times in the left margin, using a menu

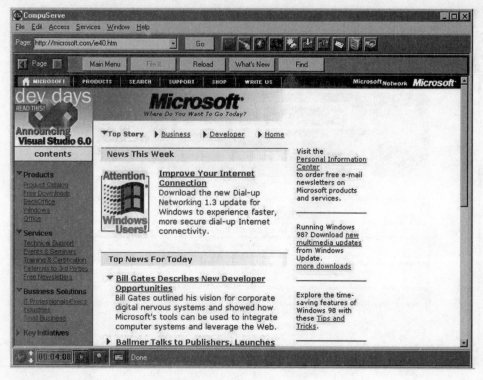

The Microsoft web site – packed with useful information, software upgrades and news

command, or a keyboard shortcut (usually Ctrl + C). Place the highlighted copy on to the PC's **Clipboard** by clicking the Copy command (usually on the edit menu) or the copy icon on the toolbar.

Now switch to the e-mail message window and insert a cursor by clicking the mouse button, and use the Paste command which can be found in the Edit menu, or you can use Ctrl + V on the keyboard. This technique also gets around the problem of formatted text, which the recipient may have difficulty in reading – they might not use the same word processor as you – if it is sent as an 'attachment' to an e-mail message. An attachment is a non-standard file, such as that created on a word processor, containing special formatting commands, like bold or italics. Such files can still be sent by e-mail, but they must be specially designated, by calling them attachments, so that the files are handled differently, to make sure that they arrive at their destination in one piece.

Pictures from a digital camera or scanner, and graphics files can only be sent as e-mail attachments. They can be very large indeed, so make sure you're using the appropriate file format and **compression** level, otherwise they will take a long time to send. You'll find a more detailed explanation in the manual or Help files supplied with the software and hardware you're using to generate or process images.

Each time you visit an Internet web site your **browser** tries to be helpful and keep a detailed record of the address, and the information you've been looking at. It's all stored away in a file called a **cache** and it's a way to reduce access time. Caches fill up quickly, consuming many megabytes of valuable hard disk space, so it's a good idea to empty it from time to time. Navigator's **cache** is in the Netscape folder and Internet Explorer stores it in the Windows 95 directory, as Temporary Internet Cache. Your **browser** may have an option to regularly empty the **cache** or limit its size, if so, it's worth using.

If you share your PC and want to keep your Internet activities private then be aware that the addresses of sites you've visited are stored in the History folder in Windows 95. Some web sites create 'cookies', which also contain addresses. **Cookies** are nothing to be worried about, they're small data files that contain information provided by you – but not your PC – that help some Internet pages to load faster. (See page 76 for a more detailed explanation.)

Internet service providers

AOL   *0800 2791234*
BT LineOne   *0345 777464*
Cable & Wireless   *0500 200980*
Claranet   *0171 903 3000*
CompuServe   *0990 000200*
Demon Internet   *0181 371 1234*
Direct Connection   *0800 0720000*
Freeserve   *01442 353000*
Global Internet   *0181 957 1041*
MSN   *0345 002000*

Netcom   *01344 395600*
Pipex Dial   *0500 474739*
Virgin Net   *0500 558800*

Q&A   Solutions to real world problems

Sounds absolutely fabulous!

Q   I see in my Windows 95 Sounds Properties (in Control Panel) there is a heading 'You've got post', but I am unable to make it work. I actually heard it once and it sounded like Joanna Lumley, but she went away, and won't come back. I assume that it refers to e-mail and would draw one's attention to waiting mail. Is it possible to implement it, and if so would one have to be connected to the Internet, or just have the computer switched on?
M.A. via e-mail

A   Ms Lumley's voice was almost certainly put onto your PC by AOL (America On Line) Internet access program. It's one of several messages recorded by the ex-Avenging comedy actress; AOL hoped she would give the UK version of their software a more British feel. Should you so desire, you can use these sound files to replace the standard Windows 95 dings, pings and ta-das. Click on the Sounds icon in Control Panel, and then choose a Windows 'event' that you want Joanna's dulcet tones to replace (e.g. asterisk, critical stop, start or exit Windows). Highlight the event, then use the browse button to find the sound file, click on it to associate it to the action, then click OK. The files are called 'Gotpost', 'Filefini', 'Welcome' and 'Goodbye' and are normally found in the AOL directory.

Image maker

Q   My two sisters live abroad and we keep in touch by e-mail. I tried to send a 'card' which I'd designed, but copying and pasting into my e-mail message resulted in only the text being transmitted. I tried copying it to various files and sending as an attachment but again, only the text parts were transmitted. Is this because the receiving software is not compatible with my MS software?

P.R. via e-mail

A   It shouldn't matter what Internet software your sisters are using; the problem is that you are trying to send a file that contains a mixture of non-standard graphics and text. The simplest solution would be to send your card as a compressed image file. If the card was created in a graphics program simply save it as a **JPEG** (.jpg) file, and send that. If it is a word processor document then you have to convert it into an image, using a graphics program like PaintShop Pro (trial versions of PSP are widely distributed on magazine cover disks). Capture the card to the **Clipboard** by pressing Print Screen on the keyboard, then paste it into PSP, where it can be edited and saved as a .jpg file.

Picture this

Q   It seems that all of the pictures I view on the Internet are recorded on my computer. They appear to be stored in Temporary Internet files, Windows History, Internet Cache and MGI PhotoSuite. Is there any way that I can avoid this happening and are there any other 'hidden' places where pictures or text may be stored?

A.T. Derby

A   Internet image and text files are usually only stored once, in the **browser cache**, the other instances you have found are cross-references and registers of the sites you've visited. You can't easily switch off this facility, but some browsers can be set to automatically empty, or limit the size of the **cache**, others you will have to delete manually. Look in your **browser's** Options or Preferences menu. The ever-helpful Tweak UI utility has a feature called Paranoia, which will clear Explorer and Windows History files every time you log on. Tweak UI can be downloaded from Microsoft at: www.microsoft.com/windows/download/powertoy.exe

Net contributions

Q Until recently I have been sending my publisher copy on floppy disks, via surface mail. Now I am planning to send copy by e-mail, using the latest AOL software. They have requested copy in text only format – why is that, and how do I go about it?

Also, how should I transmit graphics, scanned diagrams, colour photos and book covers, to be used as thumbnails for book review articles? Which available file format e.g. .bmp, .jpg, .gif, .art, .avi, etc., is used by the publishing and printing industry?
R.C. via e-mail

A A lot of freelance journalists and authors think they're doing publishers a favour by sending them formatted text documents – i.e. with bold and italic characters etc. – as e-mail attachments. It can cause problems as files have to be converted back to plain text, before they can be used for page layout. Your publisher has asked you to send text-only files so by far the simplest method would be to copy and paste text from your word processor, into the blank copy area on the AOL Write e-mail form.

You will have to talk to your publisher to find out which type of image format they prefer, but the chances are it will be .jpg or **JPEG** files. They're reasonably compact so they can be sent quickly by e-mail, and the quality is good enough for publication in magazines and newspapers.

E-mail security

Q I want to send a sensitive document to the USA, and have thought of including it as an enclosure to an e-mail. What are the risks of some-one in the UK (or anywhere else) seeing it, either deliberately or by accident? Clearly, it must go onto my ISP's server and onto the server of the recipient's ISP. How long does it stay at any of these sites, where I assume it could be vulnerable to snooping or interception? Is it deleted as soon as the recipient says 'Delete'? And how much would the use of password protection alter the vulnerability?
J.E.J. via e-mail

A Although all UK and US Internet Service Providers claim a high degree of confidentiality at their ends of an Internet connection, there is no way of knowing what route your message takes, what happens to it whilst it is in transit, and how long it remains on any of the server computers it passes through. The only safe way to send files is to **encrypt** them and provide the recipient with a 'key' to unlock the file, when it has been downloaded onto their PC. Even so, no **encryption** system is 100% secure, though some, like PGP (Pretty Good Privacy), is so good that it takes a powerful supercomputer a long time to crack it. Any person or organisation wanting to read your e-mail would have to be very determined, and very well equipped. PGP is a **freeware** program and various versions that will operate on a wide range of computers and **operating systems** are available from numerous sites around the Internet. You will find a good overview of PGP and **encryption**, plus links to various download sites at: http://www.pgpi.com

Mail binding

Q   It may be a simple question, but how long do e-mails take to arrive at their destination?
P.D. via e-mail

A   Unfortunately there is no simple answer. The vast majority of e-mails arrive at the recipient's mailbox within a few minutes of being sent, but it is not unheard of for messages to take hours, or even days to get to where they are going. Even when it gets there an e-mail will remain unread, until the recipient accesses their mailbox. Hold-ups in transit can and do occur. They're mostly caused by breakdowns, congestion on the net, and how busy the servers are at each end of the connection.

Search and rescue

Q   I am new to Internet use and wonder if you can recommend a quick method of tracing a business, when only the company name is known but not the web site address?
R.I.S. via e-mail

A   The starting point to finding anything on the net is one of the many **search engines**. There's a well-maintained site with links to all of the main ones, along with a short summary of their strengths and weaknesses at: http://www.agt.net/public/minerdb/search.htm

There's a bit of a knack to finding exactly what you want, without having to wade through hundreds of irrelevant site listings. First, choose the most appropriate **search engine** and if possible narrow the search criteria. If you're only interested in UK-based companies there's no point searching the entire World Wide Web. Carefully choose and prioritise the keywords, and avoid using vague or general words like 'computer', for example, which will elicit a huge response.

Intra-spective

Q Can you please tell me the difference, if any, between the Internet and an Intranet? I have always assumed that they were the same, and that Intranet was a misspelling of Internet. However, I have seen the word Intranet so often recently that I am having doubts.
G.A.B. Surrey

A An Intranet is a private or company computer network, which to its users looks and functions like an Internet web site. PCs use familiar **browser**-type software to access and retrieve information, by clicking on icons, buttons and highlighted links. Intranets use the same kind of system for transferring files as the Internet (known to its friends as Transmission Control Protocol over Internet Protocol or TCP/IP).

Cache 22

Q I notice that with frequent Internet use, vast numbers of files are accumulating in the **cache** sub-directory of the Mosaic directory on my computer. Do these files serve any useful purpose? Is there any disadvantage to deleting them at regular intervals to avoid them gradually using up hard disk space?
T.H. via e-mail

A They can sometimes come in handy if you've forgotten a particular web address or need to retrieve information quickly, but in the main they're just taking up space, and can be safely removed.

Nimble net

Q   Is it possible to go faster on the Internet? There are several software packages claiming to do this. How reliable and effective are they?
J.Y. via e-mail

A   The rate at which Internet data is sent to and from your computer is determined by many different things, including the speed and efficiency of the PC, **modem** and communications software, the quality of the telephone line, and even the time of day – when east-coast America wakes up at around midday, transfer speeds can slow down dramatically. The programs you've seen cannot change any of these but they can, however, make use of 'idle time'. When a data transfer is complete, the software automatically downloads other frequently-used or nominated pages, or uses a trick called forward-caching, which is loading all the links from the page you're viewing, so when you click on one of them, it appears instantly. If you're a fast reader, or there's not much on the page, or your connection is running slowly, there's little or nothing to be gained. A faster **modem** and time spent optimising your PC and Internet software will have a much bigger effect.

Credit where it's due

Q   I've just had my first month on the net and I have seen lots of sites requesting payment before membership is granted. Just how risky is it to reveal credit card details by e-mail? Other than not buying, have you any advice on this subject which should become more popular with the advent of digital, interactive, TV?
G.R. via e-mail

A   Internet fraud is possible, and it does happen, but you need to look at it in perspective, and take the view that most traders are basically honest. After all, you reveal your credit number every time you use it, whether personally in a shop or restaurant, or when buying goods and services over the phone. Have you ever wondered what happens to all those discarded slips and carbons? You can play it safe by only dealing with large, reputable companies based in the UK, many of whom use **encryption** systems on their web sites, which will prevent your card details from being intercepted as they move around the Net. These will become more commonplace as the number of on-line shopping services grows. However, for the moment, there's a simple rule of thumb. The more distant, obscure, unusual or dubious the service or product, the greater the potential risk.

Mail call

Q   Is it necessary to leave your computer switched on all the time in order to receive e-mail coming in at various times of the day?
R.W.S. Ross

A   No, your incoming e-mail is automatically stored in a personal mailbox on the service provider's computer; every time you log on to the system it will alert you to the fact that mail is waiting.

Never say never

Q   While on holiday in Canada recently, I bought a copy of Quarterdeck CleanSweep and installed it on my Gateway P5-75 (Windows 95). I failed to notice however that it had activated the 'Update-It' program, which automatically dials up the Quarterdeck web site to download software updates. It must have tried to contact Quaterdeck and failed because a message appeared in a window stating 'Network error – the server name and address could not be resolved'. Underneath was another window, which indicated an attempt to update CleanSweep's 'config' file. Clicking OK did not remove either window and they appear each time the machine is started. Setting the Update-It option to 'never' has had no effect. Any suggestions on how to remove the windows?
G.F. via e-mail

A   Quarterdeck maintain that the disobedient 'never' option is not a bug, it's just 'wrongly worded'. Figure that one out. The way to prevent CleanSweep from constantly trying to dial up the manufacturer's web site is to remove Update-It from your PC's StartUp menu. From Start on the desktop, click on Settings, then Taskbar and select Remove from the Start Menu Programs tab. Open up the StartUp folder from the directory tree, highlight Update-It, hit the Delete key and it will trouble you no more.

Private practice

Q   Is there any way of removing the list of previously visited web sites on my Internet **browser**?
T.P. via e-mail

A   In addition to the list of most recent Internet addresses or URLs (uniform resource locators), your **browser** creates several other, much more detailed records, of where you've been and what you've been looking at, including copies of actual pages. Apart from the privacy aspect – which could be important if your PC is shared with others – it takes up a lot of hard disk space. Pretty well all **browsers** maintain a **cache** file where graphics and details of pages are stored. Microsoft Internet Explorer hides its **cache** in Windows Temporary Internet Files folder; Netscape Navigator's **cache** is in the Navigator folder. Unless you actually want to keep these files it's a good idea to clear the **cache** every so often. Explorer can do this automatically; click on the View menu, then Options and Navigation.

Internet records are also stored in a History folder. Netscape for Windows 95 has its own, called netscape.hst; MS Explorer creates one in the Windows 95 directory called Temporary Internet Files; entries can be deleted by highlighting and pressing the delete key, or by dragging them to the Recycle Bin. **Cookies** are another way of finding out what you have been up to, they're small files that contain details of the workings of frequently visited sites and can be safely deleted. Explorer keeps them in the **cookies** folder in Windows, Navigator's can be found using the Find utility on the Start menu, to find it type in cookies.txt. Internet **browsers** also squirrel away Internet information in the Windows **Registry**, though unless you know what you're doing they're best left alone. Don't forget that anything you put into the Recycle Bin will remain there until it is emptied. Finally, if you're feeling really paranoid, it's worth bearing in mind that when you delete files and data from your PC, you're basically only removing the entry in a contents listing, the actual information remains on the hard disk and can still be read, until it is overwritten by new data.

Backtrack

Q In several recent movies, hackers, spooks and action heroes are shown plotting the location of an Internet user, wherever in the world they happen to be. Is that sort of thing possible?
M.D. Kent

A Probably. You can do something similar – though not quite so visually dramatic – if you have Windows 95 and Internet access. Tucked away inside Win 95 there's an interesting little program called Trace Route, that automatically logs the path of an Internet connection, as it passes around the Web, through other computers and via high-speed links and satellites, to the destination server. Open the MS-DOS window in Programs on the Start menu and at the C: prompt type 'tracert', then an Internet address (i.e. tracert www.telegraph.co.uk), press return and watch it go!

Sound and vision

Q I expect you're used to silly questions ... so here's another! Should I be able to get sound and movement from Internet sites? I think you'll probably say yes and if so, why can't I? I have a 486 PC with a recently installed CD-ROM drive, however the only time I get sound is when I play a CD or when I'm using CompuServe and am told 'You have mail waiting'. How do I activate my sound card so it works with the Internet?
R.J.R. Essex

A It's not a silly question at all. There are plenty of Internet web sites with sound and video or animated clips but the trouble is, they're not always obvious. Much also depends on how your **browser** software has been set up, your PC specification and its multimedia capabilities, and of course, the **modem** speed. It's easy to miss multimedia clips when you're page-hopping as they can take a long time to load. A good place to find out what your PC is capable of is the RealNetworks web site. There you can download the latest video and audio player software, tune in to radio stations around the world, even watch TV (though don't expect too much). Video via the Internet is shown on a small screen and movement is jerky, sometimes no more than just a succession of still pictures. Moreover, just a few seconds of moving video can swallow up megabytes of hard disk space, which your relatively old PC may not have to spare. RealNetworks home page can be found at: www.realaudio.com

The UK site is also well worth a visit, the address is: http://www.real.co.uk

Chess challenge

Q   I am a high school student and have recently acquired an Internet connection through a local cable company. I have a passion for chess and after a long search found an American server called Chess Net. I find it very satisfactory but I have since discovered that there are some functions I cannot use. Internet veterans have suggested this is because I am not using something called Telnet. What is it, and how can I use it?

J.W. Lincs

A   Telnet is a text-based Internet facility that allows you to communicate with, and control computers remotely. Access to a Telnet site will be via your Internet Service Provider, using the terminal emulation software that's included as standard with **browsers** like Microsoft Internet Explorer. (Others, like Netscape may need upgrading.) Click on the Telnet icon on the Chess.net page (http://www.chess.net), and it starts automatically. Registration and operating instructions appear when you log on, using the password 'guest'.

Picture poser

Q   I have a Windows 95 PC. When I received graphic files via e-mail, my present installation was not able to deal with them all. It can display .jpg files and I have been able to convert others through the Wang Imaging program that was part of the original package. However, I am unable to decode .tga files, whatever that means! So my question is, how or what do I do to obtain the necessary converters to deal with this and of course any other strange files that I might receive in the future? Does this problem suggest the need for standardisation with these types of graphic files?

H.J.W. via e-mail

A   At the last count there were more than sixty different graphics file formats in PC-land, including dozens of proprietary formats, specific to various programs. Fortunately only a relatively small number of them are in everyday use (.gif, .bmp and .jpg are the most frequently encountered) and they are each suited to a particular application, hence the lack of standardisation. PaintShop Pro can open, convert and save files in all of the common formats – Version 4 lists thirty-nine different types, including .tga (Truevision Targa, since you asked). **Shareware** versions of Paintshop Pro are regularly featured on magazine cover-mounted CD-ROMs, and it is available from the Jasc web site: www.jasc.com

CHAPTER 10 **Clear out the clutter**

Your PC's hard disk is like a filing cabinet – it
needs to be kept in order and tidied up every
now and again to keep it working properly.
Here we explain how it is done.

Imagine a large, well-used filing cabinet in a busy office. It starts out all clean, shiny – and empty. Gradually it fills up: at first it is fairly well ordered, with all the folders neatly arranged, but as time goes by files are removed and not always put back in the right place. Soon there's a build-up of clutter, parts of files go missing, someone or other gets them mixed up and it takes longer and longer to find what you're looking for. Does that sound familiar?

The hard disk drive in your PC is a lot like a filing cabinet; in order to keep it working smoothly it needs to be tidied up every so often. As you install and later remove software, odd bits get left behind and the file structure becomes disorganised, slowing down the time it takes for your PC to retrieve data from the disk drive. Windows 95 and 98 include two very useful utilities that can help restore some order to the disk, and get rid of at least some of the jumble of unwanted **file fragments** that take up valuable space.

If your intention is to free up disk space, now is a good time to remove unwanted programs and all the stuff those freebie magazine cover disks leave behind. Identify which programs you no longer need using Windows Explorer, but don't be tempted to simply highlight a folder and press the Delete button. This can have disastrous consequences. A lot of programs write files into folders within Windows, change start-up files and the Windows **Registry**. They tell the computer to look for programs, but if they're no longer there Windows can crash, or do all kinds of horrible things and display worrying warning messages.

Use the Add/Remove Programs utility in Control Panel to remove redundant programs – however, this only works on software specifically written for Windows 95. Some programs have their own uninstaller utility (in the program folder) – if so, use it. Better still, use an uninstaller program, like CleanSweep, WinDelete or Uninstaller. They work best if they're installed early on, as soon as possible after you've bought a new PC. They monitor each new item of software as it is installed, noting where files are stored, so they can be safely removed. Most uninstallers make compressed backups of all the files deleted, so if a problem arises they can be re-installed.

When that's done you can use the Windows 95 utilities mentioned earlier, to tidy up the disk drive. Before you start, close down any programs that are running, switch off the screen saver if you are using one and empty the Recycle Bin (assuming everything still works okay). Go to My Computer and highlight the hard disk drive icon – usually drive C: – then, without moving the pointer arrow, press the right button on your mouse and click on Properties. The first window shows a pie-chart that will give you a general idea of how much free space is left on your disk drive. Next, click the Tools tab and you will see three options. The first step is to use **Scandisk** to check the drive for errors. **Scandisk** performs a number of checks, looking through all of the files and folders on the disk for fragments of abandoned files and testing the surface of the disk for faults. Bits of old files are gathered together and deleted. If **Scandisk** finds any bad **sectors** – areas of the disk used for data storage – they are 'tagged' so they won't be used again.

To start **Scandisk** click on the Check Now button. Choose the Thorough option and check the box that says 'Automatically fix errors' then click the Start button. Depending on the size of your hard disk this can take quite a long time – half an hour or more – so it's a good idea to do it when you've finished work for the day, or at lunch time.

When **Scandisk** has finished, go back to the Tools window and click on the Defragment button. This might report that you don't need to defragment now but if the value shown is more than, say, 8%, then it is still worth doing. **Defragging** sorts out all the files and folders on your disk, re-uniting files that have got spread around, and putting them all together at the beginning of the disk. This means the read-write heads in the drive do not have to move around so much. It speeds up data access, and reduces wear and tear on the head stepper motor. (The head stepper motor is what makes the clicking sounds, when your disk drive is busy.)

Click on the Defragment Now button. If this is the first time you have defragged your drive select Advanced and choose the Full Defragmentation option. Select OK, then Start. If you like, click on the Show Details button, and watch Defrag go to work. You will actually see blocks of data being moved from around the disk to the file areas at the front of the drive. It's quite entertaining for the first few minutes, if you've got nothing better to do, though again it can take a while to complete the job. Finally, make a note in your diary or calendar to run **Scandisk** and Defrag at least once a month.

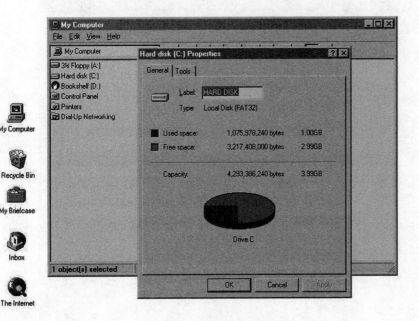

Hard Disk Properties shows you at a glance how much free space you have remaining on your disk drive

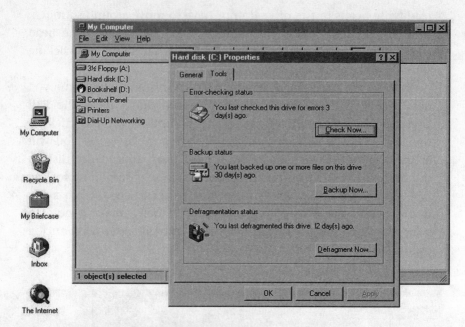

Keep your disk drive clean and free of clutter with Windows 95 and 98
disk tools and utilities

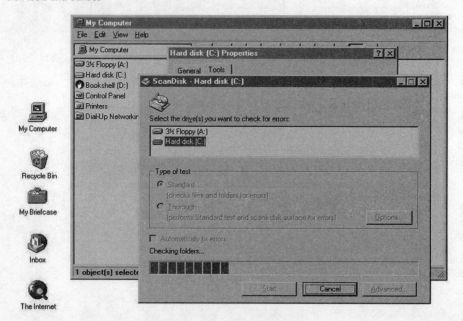

ScanDisk checks your disk drive for errors and lost file fragments

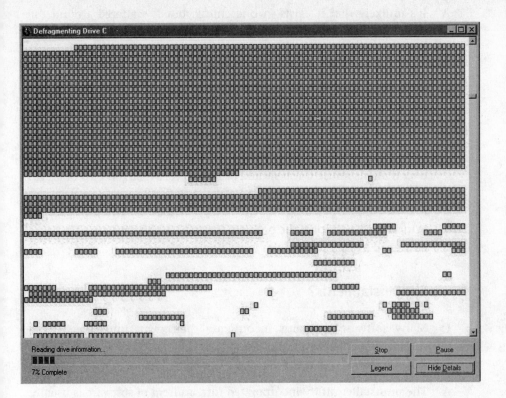

Defrag re-organises your disk drive, helping to improve the
performance of your most frequently used applications

Q&A Solutions to real world problems

Missing in action

Q   Can you please tell me where 300Mb have disappeared to on my C:
    drive. I checked all my folders and they add up to 1100Mb but
    according to my PC the remaining free space on the 2Gb hard drive
    comes to just 600Mb.
    A.N. via e-mail

A   It's unlikely that it exists in one chunk, but is scattered around the drive in various files. The free-space indicator and pie chart in Tools are not very reliable, and **compression** programs – if you're using one – can produce misleading readings. Several hundred megabytes of empty disk space can apparently 'disappear' into a swap file, which is a temporary memory created by Windows 95 and the amount changes, according to the application in use. The way disk space is allocated is another probable cause. Data is stored in clusters, but if the drive contains a lot of files that are smaller than each cluster, the space left over remains unused. You should be able to recover a few tens of megabytes by running **Scandisk** and Defrag, and don't forget to empty the Recycle Bin. Upgrading to the later version of Windows 95, or Windows 98 will solve the problem for good as they both use the more efficient **FAT** 32 filing system (see Chapter 16).

Easy instalments?

Q   Many software programs incorporate their own uninstallers. How reliable and efficient are they?
R.H. Farnham

A   The uninstaller utility incorporated into an item of software is usually the safest way to delete that program; it is regrettable that all programs don't include them as standard. The uninstaller will have a record of where all the files that were loaded by that program are located, so when it is removed it should leave nothing behind. Windows 95 keeps track of software with an uninstall facility and lists them in Add/Remove Programs in Control Panel. Removing software by simply deleting the file from the directory tree in Explorer or My Computer (or Filing Cabinet in Windows 3.x), almost always results in orphaned files. At the very least they waste valuable hard disk space; they can also interact with other programs and cause erratic operation or crashes, or worse! Programs like CleanSweep and Uninstaller are a good investment. They monitor all new installations, so they can be safely deleted when the time comes. They can also track down bits of old software left lying around. On most well-used machines they can usually recover several tens of megabytes of lost hard disk space.

Little arrows

Q   How do I get rid of those irritating little arrows in the corner of 'shortcuts' on the Windows 95 desktop? I understand it can be done by deleting a few entries in the Windows **registry**, but which ones? I'm sure I can't be the only one who is bothered by them.
P.A. Woking

A   The easiest way to do it is to use a software utility called Tweak UI. This can do all sorts of things to the way your desktop is presented, including making changes to mouse speed and sensitivity, animation, sound and document **templates**, and a lot more besides. It's available as a free download from Microsoft's web site. The following **URL** will take you directly to it: http://www.microsoft.com/windows/software/powertoy.html

Lost in space

Q   I wanted to clear out some redundant files to make room on my laptop. The most regularly used programs are Word, WinFax Pro, Pipex Dial and Netscape. In my **DOS** directory I have a growing list of files with the **extension** .tmp. Most use 0 bytes, about every fifth one has 1,506 bytes, and a few have serious numbers between 15k and 250k. Any advice about what they might be and whether I can safely dump them?
J.C. via e-mail

A   They are temporary files, created by the PC and its software for the short-term storage of data. Normally they're automatically deleted, but they can be left behind if the PC or the application locks up, or isn't closed down properly. Any file ending with .tmp (temporary) or .swp (swapfile) and starting with the tilde sign (~) can be safely deleted, though if you are using Windows 3.1 this should only be attempted from within **DOS**, when Windows is not running. You may also find a lot of left-over temporary files stored in a directory called Temp, which is normally inside Windows. Help files also take up a lot of room; check through applications to look for text documents or files ending with the extension .hlp. Whenever you delete a file or application it's a good idea to wait a day or two, before you empty the Recycle Bin, to make sure your PC is still working normally. While deleted files are still in the bin they can be restored.

Immovable icon?

Q How can I get rid of an icon on the Desktop? I installed PsiWin with my Psion 5, but found a previous version of PsiWin that conflicted with Windows 95, so I deleted the program using the Remove facility. However, I cannot get rid of the icon on Desktop. If I right click on the icon and go to Properties, it says there are none. Is there some way to get rid of it?
   G.A. via e-mail

A The PsiWin icon isn't protected, so normally you should be able to remove it by dragging it to the Recycle Bin, or highlighting it with a single mouse click, and pressing the Delete key. Occasionally icons simply refuse to go, in which case go into Explorer, open the Windows directory, then the Desktop folder, and manually delete the relevant shortcut file.

Irritating icon

Q I have an Icon on my Windows 95 Desktop called 'InBox' which stubbornly refuses to be deleted. I don't use it and can't see any point in leaving it to clutter my Desktop. When I drag it to the Recycle Bin it comes up with a yellow circle with a diagonal line across it, which I presume is telling me that I can't delete it. Is there a way of removing it?
   T.G. via e-mail

A The InBox icon is protected. It opens Microsoft Exchange e-mail and messaging utilities, which is an integral part of a standard Windows 95 installation. There are ways of removing the icon that involve tinkering with the Windows 95 **registry**, but it's not something we would recommend – even experienced users can get themselves into trouble. The safest way to remove it is to delete Exchange from your system. From the Start menu click on Settings, then Control Panel, and Add/Remove Programs. Click on the Windows Set-Up tab, check Microsoft Exchange, then click on Details. Check the two boxes and then select OK. When you restart your PC the InBox icon will be no more. You can easily re-install Exchange from the Windows 95 CD-ROM at any time, using the Add/Remove Program utility.

Flying the flag

Q Microsoft doesn't miss a trick in promoting its own image, even to the detriment of its captive customers. My latest gripe is that 'Flying Windows' is the only screen saver that can be individually installed/ uninstalled on my machine. I prefer 'Flying through Space' because it is far less distracting when I'm working at my desk. I would therefore like to uninstall all the rest to save space, but they seem to come as a job lot, apart from the flag-waving 'Flying Windows'. Is there any way of sorting this out?
K.R. via e-mail

A You can easily delete unwanted screen savers using the Find utility. It's on the Start menu, click on it, then the Name & Location tab and in the field marked Look In, type C:\Windows. Next, select the Advanced tab and in the Of Type field enter 'screen saver' and click Find Now. A list of the Windows 95 screen savers on your system should then appear below. Highlight the ones you want to get rid of, hit the Delete button on your keyboard and they'll be sent to the Recycle Bin. If for any reason you want to get them back again they can be re-installed from the Windows 95 CD-ROM, using the Add/Remove utility in Control Panel.

Missing sound

Q I am running Office 97 and Windows 95, and had installed a sound card before, but I had to format the hard drive to install them as I was running an old version of Ami Pro. Now I find that my sound card does not work, and have been told by my computer guru friend that a command needs to be entered. Please could you tell me if this is right, and, whether it is or it isn't, what do I do to get the sound back?
R.F. via e-mail

A Reformatting your hard disk is a drastic way to get rid of Ami Pro! Next time use more conventional measures to remove unwanted software. You've lost the **driver** for your sound card so call up the Install/ Remove Hardware **wizard** in Control Panel. This should automatically identify the sound card and try to locate a suitable **driver**. If it can't find one it will ask you to supply the **driver** on disk. One should have been supplied with the PC, or with the sound card, if it was bought separately. If you haven't got it you should be able to obtain one from the PC vendor, or failing that, the sound card manufacturer. Most of them have Internet web sites with **driver** libraries, although you will have to find out the make and model number first.

Coming clean

Q Can an uninstaller program remove applications that were installed before it was installed, if you see what I mean? The ones I have looked at suggest that the uninstaller has to be running when an application is put on the computer, so that they know how to remove the programs that I wish I'd never installed. How can I uninstall software that the Windows 95 uninstaller does not give me the option of uninstalling? Help.
M.C. via e-mail

A When you have an uninstaller program running on your system it monitors new software, noting where the files are stored, so they can be completely removed when necessary. Nevertheless, uninstallers do also work retrospectively, as it were, though there's a chance some bits of a program may be left behind. However, these 'orphaned' files should be found by the clean-up utilities included on most uninstallers.

Wipe the slate

Q I have asked six different computer professionals whether deleting items from the Recycle Bin in Windows 95 renders them irrecoverable by any means. Three of them say yes but the others say no, and that with the right software the information can be retrieved. Apparently, to make such information irrecoverable requires a program to fully destroy it. Who is right? Can you recommend a program that wipes information permanently if it is not possible by normal deletion?
T.S. Sussex

A When you delete a file on a PC all you're really doing is removing the entry in the hard disk drive's table of contents. The **operating system** then regards it as free space but the original data remains, until it has been overwritten by another application. Up until that point it can still be recovered. There are several programs that will fully erase latent files, usually by replacing them with random data. One of the best known is a **shareware** utility called Blackboard File Wipe. It pops up from time to time on magazine cover CD-ROMs, or it can be downloaded from various web sites around the Internet, including: http://www.softseek.com

Missing links

Q   What are DLL files? I currently have 1,296 of them on my laptop – what do they do?
V.D. via e-mail

A   DLL stands for Dynamic Link Library. They're a family of files that contain programming code, bitmap images, icons and other resources that can be shared by one or more applications. Some of them can be quiet large and it's not unusual for a PC to end up with lots of duplicate and redundant DLLs, left behind by deleted programs and it is therefore possible that some of the 1,300 odd files on your machine are wasting valuable hard disk space. However, mess with DLLs at your peril! Do not be tempted to erase any of them without first making absolutely sure they're not being used. The only safe way to do that is with a disk cleaner program.

CHAPTER 11 **Mice, joysticks and steering wheels**

When it comes to choosing a mouse or a joystick, do not be swayed by fancy features. The key is to find something that you will be comfortable with.

Although your PC came with a mouse don't feel you are stuck with it – there are plenty of other ways of moving the pointer around the screen, and making things happen. In fact you don't even need a mouse at all, which is worth knowing if your rodent expires or suddenly stops moving. On the Windows 95 desktop, and in most programs you can select icons or menu items by pressing the Alt or Tab keys on the keyboard, and move through the selections using the cursor arrows, confirming your choice with the Enter/Return key.

It's also possible to move the mouse pointer from the keyboard. Some Windows 95 keyboards have the facility already built-in, other- wise it can be enabled from the Accessibility icon in Control Panel. Click on the mouse tab – assuming your mouse is still working – check the Use Mousekeys box and then the Settings button. There you will find a second check box for the keyboard shortcut, that will allow you to switch between the mouse and keyboard mouse control using the numerical keypad.

Nowadays mice come in all sorts of weird and wonderful shapes, so if you find yours uncomfortable or difficult to use it's worth trying a few others for size. Don't forget, if the pointer moves too quickly you can slow it down. Just click on the mouse icon in Control Panel, select the Motion tab and adjust the speed slider to suit.

Most PC mice have two buttons; some have three, but don't let that bother you. Very few applications make use of the centre button, and

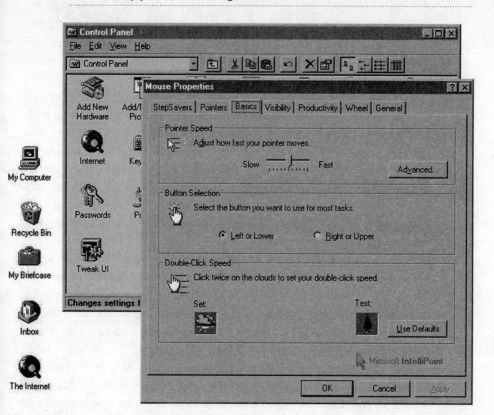

Customise your mouse – you can control the way it behaves by clicking
on the mouse icon in Control Panel

those that do normally provide a keyboard alternative. Wheel mice are
a relatively new innovation; the wheel, or roller, makes it easier to
scroll through long documents and switch between open applications.
They're a boon for word processing, especially on fast multimedia PCs,
where high-speed graphics make it difficult to move copy and paste
blocks of text.

A standard mouse is fine for most applications but they do have their
limitations. For those with joint and muscle disorders, or limited
movement in their hands, they can be difficult to use. A trackball is the
best alternative, which is a bit like a large upside-down mouse except
that they remain stationary, whilst the user moves a large ball. They
can be a bit tricky at first, especially if you're used to a mouse, but once

you get used to it they can be fast and accurate. Trackballs take up less space too, which can be an advantage on a crowded desktop, but they are dearer than an ordinary mouse with the cheapest models costing from around £40 upwards.

It is very difficult to draw accurately with a mouse. Most designers and artists prefer to use a graphics tablet, also known as digitising pads or bitpads. A hand-held stylus, in contact with a touch-sensitive pad controls cursor movement and menu selections. For a lot of people it's a far more natural way to draw and manipulate images. The smallest graphics tablets are about the size of a paperback book, with an area the size of a sheet of A5 paper; serious models are between A4 and A2. Prices start at less than £100 and rise quickly to several thousand pounds for professional models.

Touchpads or Glidepoints are a common feature on laptop PCs and are effectively miniature graphics tablets. Pointer motion is controlled by finger movement on a small touch-sensitive pad. They're now available as alternatives to a mouse or trackball, although like graphics tablets and trackballs they cost a good deal more and you can expect to pay at least £45 for one.

Virtually all pointing devices plug into the standard mouse port or serial communications socket, so they are very easy to fit. Standard mouse **driver** software is included in Windows 95, but more elaborate and exotic devices usually come with their own **drivers** on a floppy disk. Windows 95 should detect a new non-standard mouse as soon as it is plugged in, though you may need to run the Install New Hardware utility in Control Panel, to configure it properly.

A joystick is almost mandatory to play most new PC action games. You may be able to use a mouse and keyboard instead but they're a very poor substitute. Joysticks have their own dedicated connector called a Gameport which is often incorporated into the PC's sound card on the back of the main box. Joysticks are enabled from the Game Controller icon in Control Panel. Windows 95 has a good selection of **driver** software included as standard, however many joysticks come with their own installation software. If your model isn't included simply click on the Add button on the Game Controller window and follow the instructions.

Game controllers come in a bewildering range of styles and dedicated game-players fiercely debate their relative merits, but for

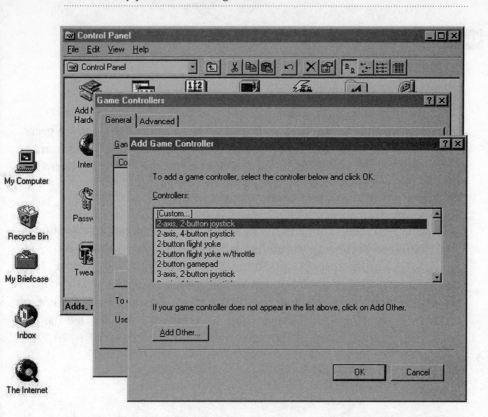

If you're using a joystick make sure it is configured properly; click on the joystick icon in Control Panel

most people comfort is more important than fancy features, which relatively few games or software packages may support. Force-feedback is a case in point. The joystick moves or vibrates under the influence of small servos built into the base of the joystick and is controlled by the game software.

Racing car game and flight simulation aficionados favour highly specialised controls, to make their game-play feel even more authentic. They include steering wheels, control yolks, even handlebars, and for added realism they can be combined with pedals and rudder bars. Needless to say they're also expensive – a good Formula 1 steering wheel and pedal set will set you back the thick end of £150!

Q&A Solutions to real world problems

Leftist tendency

Q Is it possible to purchase a left-handed keyboard? By that I mean everything after the Return/Enter key, specifically the arrow and number keys, which are normally on the right hand side of the keyboard, on the left. Do you know if such a device is available?
S.B. via e-mail

A The Keyboard Company stocks a wide range of specialist and purpose-designed keyboards, including a left-handed model – product code KBC 3500 – which costs £81 (including VAT), plus post and packaging. They can also supply a left-handed mouse, which costs £57. The Keyboard Company can be reached at: 07000 500515. The mail-order division of the Anything Left-Handed shop in London also sells left-handed computer keyboards (£100); their telephone number is 0181 770 3722.

Sticking point

Q Do you know of anyone who makes a keyboard that I could use with my Gujerati language word processor? Ideally each key would have standard English letters as well. I have thought of placing stickers over the keys on a normal QWERTY keyboard, but there must be a better way.
A.J.S. London

A Several companies produce custom-engraved keys and specialist keyboards to order. All you have to do is provide them with a character design and layout. Access Keyboards charge between £1 and £2 per key and they would expect a fully prepared keyboard to cost in the region of £40 to £50. Normal delivery time is between two to four weeks and they can be reached on 01734 663333. One-off custom-engraved keyboards from Contech Keyboards normally cost from £60 to £70 but they quoted us a delivery time of just one week from the receipt of an order. Their phone number is 01438 315757.

Maplin Electronics have a range of plug-in I/O controller cards, switching devices and control software. They can be reached at 01702 554000.

Tingle factor

Q I have a Packard Bell 486 PC and my wife, who is a writer, has an Olympia electronic typewriter. On both of these machines she is having serious problems, apparently from static electricity, with tingling in the toes, fingers and face, which I do not feel. We have tried an earthed wrist strap and an earthed wire taped to the typewriter case. She has tried wearing plastic, rubber, cotton and leather gloves. Some gave protection for a while, but they all failed eventually. My local computer shop has been unable to offer any useful advice – do you have any suggestions?
M.P. Edinburgh

A Static electricity seems an unlikely candidate. The symptoms you describe are very similar to those experienced by sufferers of repetitive strain injury or RSI and so your wife should consult her GP if the condition persists. RSI has become a growing problem with the advent of electronic keyboards. They permit much faster typing speeds than mechanical and electric typewriters; moreover the keys tend to have shorter strokes, often with little or no cushioning. Over time the constant jarring can result in damage to joints in the fingers and hand. There are many ways to avoid and alleviate the condition, including relatively simple measure like a change in posture or seating, to ergonomically designed keyboards. There's an abundance of information on RSI on the net and an excellent overview, along with plenty of helpful tips can be found at: http://www.eecs.harvard.edu/rsi

Lost for words

Q I am a postgraduate student having to type up long texts, albeit very slowly. This takes up a great deal of research time. Would any of the voice packages help? Are they effective for academic work?
P.B. via e-mail

A Voice typing software is improving all the time, and it is a boon to those who cannot, for one reason or another, use a PC keyboard.

However, even the best of them are still very slow, even compared with a novice typist. They suffer from a number of drawbacks. Firstly they have to be taught to recognise your voice and at first they make a lot of mistakes, which have to be corrected manually, which is, of course, time consuming. If you catch a cold or lose your voice they become even more unreliable. They're not very good at discriminating between a voice and background noise, so you'll probably have to wear a headset, and work in comparative silence. Whilst they can become quite proficient with ordinary, everyday words, the kind of work you're doing will almost certainly involve lots of obscure words, technical jargon and acronyms. Each time you use a new one it will have to be keyed in. Typing skills can be developed quite quickly; they improve rapidly with practice and will be of lasting value throughout your career. There are several good typing tutorial packages on the market including the old favourite, Mavis Beacon Teaches Typing. http://www.mavisbeacon.com

Scroll control

Q   I have a P133 with 32Mb of **RAM** and a 1.7Mb hard drive. All was well until I replaced the original video card with a 2Mb card made by Video Excel. It has made a noticeable improvement to the speed of video games but has created unexpected problems in Microsoft Word 6. There has been a huge increase in scrolling speed. It's most acute when dragging and dropping a block of highlighted text – more often than not it goes sailing past the place I want it to go, ending up at the top or bottom of the document. I've searched through all of the control panels and menu options in Word, to find a way of slowing it down, but without success. Do you have any suggestions?
R.L. Sussex

A   It has more to do with Windows than Word. Right click on My Computer, then Properties, select Performance then the Graphics tab. If the acceleration slider is set to Full, move it to None. This is only a temporary fix, though, and you will have to move it back when you want to play games. If your mouse has its own utility software, you may find there's an acceleration control; the one in Control Panel won't make any difference. A longer-term solution would be to get a 'wheel' mouse, such as those made by Microsoft, Logitech and Trust. The wheel is usually located between the right and left buttons and is operated by the index finger, allowing the user to scroll through a document, dragging and dropping copy at any speed.

On the line

Q   I want to use a computer to run a model railway. I can program in Pascal and BASIC and have access to a range of PCs (8086, 386 and Pentium). Can you tell me where I can find out more about interfacing the computer to the layout?
L.K. Herts

A   Your first port of call – or should that be station? – is the Model Electronic Railway Group, who have developed several systems for controlling model railways, and signalling systems, using various types of computer – apparently Sinclair Spectrums are very popular. There are also a number of off-the-shelf software packages, interface boards and even model trains with built-in controller chips, that will run on almost any type of PC. The Model Electronic Railway Group have prepared an information pack about themselves – to receive a copy, send two first class stamps to: Paul King, 25 Fir Tree Way, Hassocks, West Sussex BN6 8BU, or give them a call on (01273) 844530. If you have an Internet connection you will find a vast amount of information plus links to other useful sites at: http://www. magic.ca/~prodyn/resources.html

Controlling interest

Q   I am interested in hooking up non-IT kit to a PC, to open and close doors, curtains, alarms, garage doors, videos, cameras etc. Do you know of any companies or web sites that I can contact?
S.P. via e-mail

A   If you're handy with a soldering iron and know your way around a circuit diagram then it's well worth visiting: http://www.hut.fi/Misc /Electronics/Circuits/parallel_output.html
   There you will find details of how to build a simple interface circuit

that connects to your PC's parallel port, to operate a relay or switching device. There's also software and programming information, plus links to other related sites. Information about a PC control system that can operate almost every appliance in your home can be found at: http://ourworld.compuserve.com/homepages/mark_gilmore_2

CHAPTER 12 **Scanners and digital cameras**

If you want to get artwork and pictures into your PC then you need a scanner or a digital still camera.

Getting photographs into a PC used to be incredibly difficult. As recently as five years ago it was almost impossible, without access to eye-wateringly expensive peripherals. It's also worth remembering that the PCs of the early 1990s (mostly 386 and 486 machines with 8Mb of memory or less) were only barely capable of displaying and processing high quality colour pictures. That's all changed, for today's Pentium PCs are cheaper, faster and vastly better equipped to handle photographic images. Competent colour scanners now sell for less than £50 and digital still cameras are not far behind – we'll be looking at them in more detail later on.

But first colour scanners, and why your life is incomplete without one. A scanner is arguably the most versatile computer peripheral yet devised. It will enable you to load high quality photographs and images into your PC, for incorporation into documents, presentations, newsletters and Internet web pages. Most models also come with a suite of utility software that can turn your computer into a sophisticated photo studio, colour photocopier, fax machine and document reader.

First generation scanners were cumbersome to install and use but most recent ones, including many current budget models, can be up and running in a matter of minutes. There are basically two types of general-purpose scanner, utilising two sorts of PC connection. Most non-specialist models are either flatbed or sheet-feed; a few hand-held models are still available but they're virtually obsolete now. A flatbed scanner looks like a small photocopier. The image or document is placed face down on a glass plate or 'platen' and scanned by a moving image sensor, on the other side of the glass. On a sheet-feed scanner the image sensor is static, the document moves past it, drawn through a set of rollers, rather like a fax machine. Flatbeds can take up a lot of desk space but they are able to scan unwieldy objects like books or irregularly shaped items. Sheet-feed scanners are usually a lot smaller or incorporated into multi-function devices like combined printers and fax machines, but they can only cope with a single sheet of paper.

Scanners either come with their own interface card or they connect to the PC's printer port. The former means you will have to open up your PC, and it must have a vacant card slot on the **motherboard** for the **SCSI** card. They tend to be more expensive too but they're also slightly quicker, however, scan speed is largely irrelevant. Unless you're planning to regularly process large numbers of images, saving a few seconds is hardly important. Parallel port scanners are suitable for 95% of home and office applications, the only minor limitation being that you cannot scan and print at the same time, even though the printer remains connected to the PC via a 'through port' on the back of the scanner.

Scanner resolution creates a lot of confusion. Resolution is a measure of how much fine detail the scanner can capture. The only figure that counts is optical resolution, which is typically quoted as a set of two numbers, i.e. 300×600 or 600×1200 dots per inch (dpi). The first figure indicates how many light sensitive elements or pixels there are on the scanner pickup head that traverses the image or document. The second number shows how many vertical 'lines' can be scanned by the pickup head, as it steps along the picture or document.

The important point to bear in mind is that most applications – where the scanned image will be shown on a PC monitor screen, or printed out by an **inkjet** printer – call for a resolution of between 100 and 200dpi. Good quality colour photographs may go up to 300dpi, but only a handful of professional applications need 600dpi or above. A lot of budget scanners claim to be able to resolve 2400×4800dpi, or more, but that is an 'interpolated' figure, which basically means the software guesses at what's in between the actual scanned dots. A lot of the time it gets it wrong and interpolated scans can look soft or slightly blurry. Another point to bear in mind is that higher resolution scans take longer and use up more hard disk space and memory to store and manipulate the image. A 4×6 inch colour photograph scanned at 2400dpi would swallow up several hundred megabytes of memory.

A scanner is heavily dependent on its operating software. All models require a **driver** program, the most common one being **TWAIN**, which operates in the background, usually from within the scanner's user interface. This normally features a preview window – showing a small thumbnail version of the scanned image – plus a set of control buttons. The **driver** automatically adjusts brightness, colour and contrast (manual controls are usually there if you need them), all you have to do is select the resolution and the task, i.e. picture acquisition, copier, fax, document reader etc. Incidentally, Windows 95 comes with a simple scanning utility. It's called Imaging and can be found in the Accessories folder on the Programs menu.

Most scanner operating programs have the facility to make a fast preview scan, to check orientation and alignment etc. before the full scan. When it has finished, the image is automatically routed to the appropriate application. For example, if it's a photograph, the picture will appear in an open window on the desktop of the selected graphics program. If it's a fax, the scanned document opens your fax software and a document to be converted into text first passes through an optical character recognition (**OCR**) utility where it is converted into a text file, which can be read by your PC's word processor. Most scanners come bundled with graphics and **OCR** programs, though more often than not they're 'lite' versions with a limited range of features.

Before you rush out and buy a scanner, there's a couple of points to bear in mind. Scanners work best with fast Pentium PCs and Windows 95 or 98 – the faster the better! If you're using an old 486, forget it, no matter what it says on the scanner box. Scanners also need lots of memory and hard disk space – you should reckon on at least 32Mb of **RAM**, (64Mb is better still) and several hundred spare megabytes on the hard drive.

Digital cameras

Fading, blurred and out of focus pictures first started coming back from the chemists almost two hundred years ago. The chemists concerned were Sir Humphry Davy and Thomas Wedgwood, who outlined the basic principles of chemical photography in the *Journal of the Royal Institution* back in 1802.

And so it was until 1981, when Sony unveiled the first prototype electronic still camera, called Mavica. It used a solid-state image sensor instead of film, and recorded images on a miniature floppy disk. Pictures could be displayed directly on a TV, sent down telephone wires or printed out on paper. Electronic still photography finally came of age during the mid 1990s when the first low-cost digital still cameras (DSCs) started to appear.

Digital still cameras still have some way to go to match the performance and price of film cameras but the pace of development is nothing short of phenomenal, so what can they do for you? Well, don't throw away your 35mm or APS compact just yet, but if you've got a reasonably up to date Pentium PC and a colour printer, a DSC can be an extremely useful and entertaining peripheral. They're a fast and efficient way of capturing images, to illustrate documents, newsletters, presentations and Internet web pages. You can use them to create personalised calendars, greetings cards, PC background icons, photo identity cards and to send pictures to relatives abroad, in fact you can use a DSC for any application where you need to get an image into a PC. The list is endless.

The benefits of DSC photography are many and varied. There's no waiting for prints to be processed; many current models have built-in LCD viewing screens so you can compose the shot and check the image straight away, and if necessary re-shoot. Running costs are minimal, there's no film to buy (though some DSCs do get through batteries at an alarming rate). Storage capacity is increasing all the time, DSCs typically capture between fifty and a hundred images on internal memory chips or cards and they can be downloaded onto the PC's hard disk at any time.

Most current models look and work exactly like a compact 35mm camera, and they're just as easy to use, simply point and shoot. DSCs with manual exposure systems and interchangeable lenses are available too, though expect to pay for the privilege. Virtually all DSCs come with PC and Mac connection kits that include a serial transfer lead – it plugs into one of the COM sockets on the back of the PC – and a suite of operating sofware. In most cases that comprises a capture and photo album utility, for retrieving and storing images, plus one or more graphics programs. These have **templates** for calendars, greetings cards and posters, plus utilities for editing photographs, special effects, correcting faults, like red-eyed and colour imbalance and adjusting brightness and contrast. In short, the software gives you the kind of creative control over your photographs normally only possible in a well-equipped film-processing lab.

So what's the catch? The two problem areas are price and picture quality. Budget and mid-range DSCs typically sell for between £250 and £400 but prices are falling rapidly and industry pundits expect there should soon be a good choice of cameras costing £150 or less. Theoretically the price has even further to fall and the first sub £100 DSCs will appear soon. Of course you have to take into account the cost of a PC and a decent colour printer, if you want hard copies and permanent storage, but it is likely that most prospective DSC owners will already have a computer.

Picture quality on first generation DSCs was quite poor. Resolution – the ability to capture fine detail – and colour accuracy are mainly determined by the number of light sensitive picture elements or 'pixels', in the **CCD** (charged coupled device) imaging chip. Early models typically had sensor grids containing just a few thousand pixels (320×240 or 480×320). The current norm is 640×480, which is equivalent to a VGA PC display and sufficient for most applications but an increasing number of mid-market cameras are now up to XGA standard, using so-called 'megapixel' sensors with 1024×960 and 1280×960 pixel arrays.

The trade-off with resolution is storage capacity but the cost of memory chips is tumbling too. Moreover a growing number of cameras use advanced **compression** techniques, such as **JPEG**, to reduce the size of the image files, without unduly affecting quality.

Setting up the capture utility on a Windows 95 PC normally takes just a few minutes. Most camera software is supplied on CD-ROM and uses automatic 'Plug and Play' installation routines to load the programs, configure the COM port, and establish the link with the camera. After that it takes just a couple of mouse clicks to view the contents of the camera's memory. To speed up the process, most capture programs download a set of thumbnail or preview images, which takes just a few seconds, you can then click on the images you want to retrieve in order to load a full-sized picture. A bitmap file can take up to a minute to download, depending on the camera and PC. Uncompressed images also take up a lot of room – several tens of megabytes – so you will need plenty of free hard disk space on your PC. However, it's a relatively simple matter to compress files using the supplied software, or programs such as PaintShop Pro or MGI Photo Suite (supplied with a lot of DSCs) which have file conversion facilities.

The software included with a digital camera allows you to quickly download images onto your PC

Some DSCs bypass the serial link connection by using removable memory cards. These postage-stamp sized modules fit into special **PC** cards that slot into expansion sockets on the sides of laptop and notebook PCs; the same modules can also be used in floppy disk adaptors, that can be read by a normal 3.5-inch disk drive. A handful of cameras have infrared communication systems that transmit data to

Your PC can hold thousands of images and programs like this one help
you to file them in an easy to use library system

suitably equipped PCs and printers. However, cameras with IR
communication links tend to be part of a single-make system, and
often only work with compatible devices from the same manufacturer.

Megapixel camera performance is getting close to photographic film –
especially when used in conjunction with the latest photorealistic colour
inkjet printers. It can certainly be good enough for many domestic
applications and if the present rate of development continues, film
cameras for home use could be on the way out within five years! See for
yourself – most PC dealers are only too pleased to give demonstrations.
If you're thinking of buying a DSC, and quality is an issue, then you
should shortlist megapixel models, or wait for prices to come down. The
market and the technology are moving very quickly, so keep an eye on
computer magazines for the latest buying advice.

Q&A   **Solutions to real world problems**

Negative attitude

Q Is it possible to scan glass negatives into a computer? I have tried using a hand-held scanner in conjunction with a light box and various coloured filters, but the contrast is too great. The proprietary transparency scanners on the market all seem to be designed to accommodate standard framed 35mm slides which are of course the wrong size, as well as being more robust than these very old glass plates. The pictures are all of the New Forest area, taken in the pre- and immediate post-war period and I hope to be able to print them out for local historians.
P.N. via e-mail

A Try using a flatbed scanner. It is possible to achieve excellent results from black and white film negatives, using a low-cost colour scanner, including models costing less than £100. On some models you may need to place a sheet of white paper behind the negative if the hinged top cover has a black coloured inner surface. The bundled software usually includes brightness and contrast adjustments, along with negative/positive conversion.

False start

Q So far I have tried three scanners and returned them all, uninstalling the software provided. However, on start up I now get a message that Windows can't find the scanner. It refers to system.ini. and another file I don't recognise. I can and do 'press any key to continue' as requested during start-up but it is a nuisance. I have now installed an HP 5100C scanner, which works, but I would like to get Windows 95 back to normal. Any help would be appreciated.
R.H. via e-mail

A It sounds as though you didn't fully uninstall those earlier scanner programs and they've left odd files and system changes behind to confuse Windows 95. Unless you are adept at editing system files it's probably easiest to use an uninstaller program to hunt down and safely delete those orphaned files (see Chapter 10).

Port whine

Q   I have just purchased a UMAX 1210P scanner. As soon as I loaded the software and rebooted the computer, the mouse stopped working and the screen saver came on and wouldn't go away. The manual seems to indicate that I need to upgrade the printer port to an EPP interface. What does it mean and which is easier? Isn't it appalling that even with a recently bought computer, Windows 95 and a relatively new scanner, I still can't get started? What happened to Plug and Play?
L.T. via e-mail

A   The EPP (Extended Parallel Port) setting on your PC allows a higher data rate. Fortunately it's a relatively simple matter to set up, though it will involve you making a small change to the **BIOS** (Basic Input Output System) program that configures your PC every time it is switched on. To access the **BIOS** look for a message such as 'press DEL to enter set-up', when the PC boots up. When the **BIOS** menu screen appears, look for an option called Chipset Features, or Integrated Peripherals and select it using the up/down arrow keys, or the mouse pointer, if it's working – the instructions for making menu selections are normally at the bottom of the display. Now look for a line that says Parallel Port, Onboard Parallel Port or Parallel Port Mode. The adjacent setting will probably say normal or standard. Highlight the line and change the selection, normally by using the Page Up and Down keys. Do not change anything else! Press Escape and that should take you back to the main menu, where you can select the Save Changes and Exit option. Select OK or Yes and the machine will continue to boot up as normal.

Lens lore

Q   I have a reasonably new PC and I am interested in buying a digital camera but I am a little mystified by the lenses that they use. Most of the ones I've seen have a focal length of 5mm to 10mm, which on my SLR camera would produce a wrap-around 'fish-eye' effect. Surely this isn't the case on digital cameras, but can they be compared with 35mm SLR type lenses?
E.M. via fax

A   The lenses on most digital cameras are equivalent to SLR lenses with a focal length of between 40mm and 50mm. The apparent disparity is due to the difference in size between a frame of 35mm film, and the CCD image sensors used in a digital camera. Most models use CCDs that are only 7mm to 10mm across, hence the need for lenses with a much shorter focal length.

Snap happy

Q   I am contemplating the purchase of my first PC with which I intend to produce illustrated documents, containing copies of photographs I have taken. It occurs to me that it may be possible for a digital camera to double as a scanner, as well as taking normal photographs thus avoiding the expense of a separate scanner. I know very little about the comparative resolution capabilities of digital cameras, so your comments would be welcome.
K.T. Leicestershire

A   An interesting idea but unfortunately the resolution of all but the most expensive digital cameras is well below that of the cheapest scanners. Even if you splashed out on a high resolution digital camera and a copy stand (£2,000 plus), the quality would still not be good enough for document scanning, whereby printed text can be read by optical character recognition (**OCR**) software and converted into a word processor file. Even budget scanners have this very useful facility. Since one of your main aims is to import existing photographs into documents created on the PC, a desktop flatbed scanner is by far the quickest, simplest and cheapest method, and you can continue to use your film camera to take photographs. The only real benefit of a digital camera in this kind of application is speed. You don't have to wait for the film to be developed, although with many shops now offering a 1-hour processing service, this is hardly a major saving. Digital cameras are improving in leaps and bounds but it's worth pointing out that pictures taken on a £5 disposable camera still contain vastly more detail than even the best digital cameras can manage at present.

Mono type?

Q   Scanner and printer manufacturers extol the virtues of their machines when dealing with colour photos but I have the problem of producing copies of old monochrome photos suitable for use in newsletters. Can you give some advice on optical resolution and the best type of machine to use?

D.B. via e-mail

A   Most low-cost colour flatbed scanners – selling for around £100 or less – will do a really good job of processing monochrome images. Optical resolution on budget models is typically 300×600dpi (dots per inch), which should be more than adequate for a newsletter. Almost all scanners can increase the apparent detail in the image, using a technique called interpolation. Basically the software fills in the gaps between the dots, giving resolutions of 600×1200dpi, and beyond.

CHAPTER 13 **Faxing from your PC**

*Why buy a fax machine when you already
have one? You can easily turn your PC into a
sophisticated fax machine – and here we tell
you how.*

It is surprising how many people spend several hundred pounds on a
desktop fax machine, without ever realising that they already have
one. Virtually any PC with a **modem** attached can send and receive
faxes, and there's nothing more to buy if you have Windows 95. We'll
begin by showing you how to enable the facility and send a fax; later
on we'll be looking at bells, whistles and add-ons.

As usual there are one or two small points to bear in mind. Unlike a
dedicated fax machine, which works all the time, you will have to
leave your PC switched on, with the fax software running if you want
to receive incoming faxes automatically, though there are ways around
that. Moreover, unless you also have a scanner or digital camera, you
are limited to sending text documents or images that have been
created on the PC, or imported as files but again that needn't be a
problem.

On the plus side there's the advantage of plain-paper operation as
you use your PC printer to make hard copies of incoming faxes. That's
if you decide to print them out as of course there's no reason why you
should, when you can view them perfectly well on the monitor screen,
and file them on disk for safe keeping, saving paper and further
reducing running costs. Faxing from a PC is faster and more efficient,
and it can be cheaper too, but more about that later on.

For home and small business users there is absolutely no reason to
buy fax software. Apart from the freebie program that is included with
Windows 95, most PCs come fitted with a **modem**, and modems sold
separately, usually come with a suite of software. You can also fax

directly from word processor programs, such as Word, WordPro and even WordPad, which is included with Windows 95. You'll find **templates** and ready-made cover sheets in New on the File menu in Word and many other advanced word processors. Voice **modems** – i.e. models designed to handle speech as well as data – also come with sophisticated answering machine utilities.

If you're wondering why you haven't come across any fax programs on your PC it's probably either because none was loaded when Windows or the **modem** was installed, or you simply haven't been looking in the right place. If Microsoft Fax is installed on your machine it can be found by clicking on the Start button, then Programs and Accessories. If it is not there, open Control Panel and click on the Add/Remove Programs icon. Select the Windows Setup tab and check the box marked Microsoft Fax. You will then be asked if you want to add all of the components, click Yes and follow the instructions. This normally involves loading the Windows 95 CD-ROM, so make sure you have it to hand. The fax handling utility on older versions of Windows 95 is contained within Microsoft Exchange; on later releases it is called Windows Messaging. The functionality is generally the same however.

Once Microsoft Fax is installed you have a number of options for sending documents. If you just want to send a few lines of text the simplest method is to open Exchange and then the InBox folder. On later versions of Windows 95 click on the InBox icon or Programs, then Accessories, then Fax, finally select the Compose New Fax icon and this will start a **wizard** program. In all cases you will be asked to enter the recipient's fax telephone number, with the option to add it to an address book, followed by a choice of themed cover pages (Urgent, Confidential, etc.). Clicking Next presents you with a text window, where you can write your message. When you have finished, click on Finish and the fax will be sent. To make your faxes look more profes-sional, you can customise the cover page. To do so choose the Cover Page Editor which will enable you to include your company name and details, plus those of the recipient, along with any other information you deem to be important.

You can also send faxes from Windows InBox. Click on the Compose menu and select New Fax and it will take you to the Microsoft Fax **wizard**. For longer or more detailed documents it is usually more

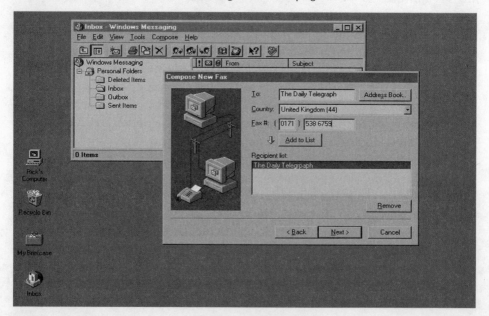

If you haven't got the Microsoft Fax program on your PC you will have to
load it from the Windows 95 or 98 CD-ROM using Add/Remove programs

Sending a fax is easy – all you have to do is enter a few basic details,
and away it goes

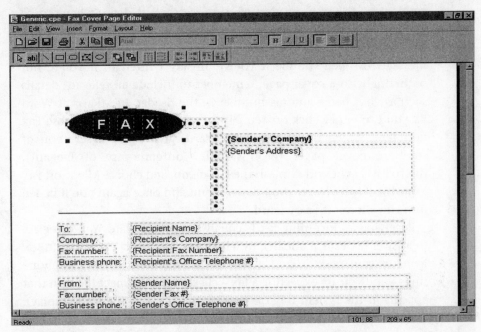

Cover Page Editor helps you to create professional looking faxes

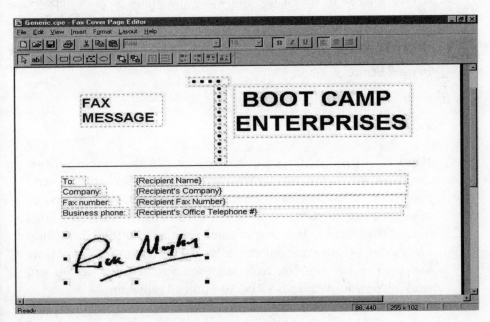

Add a signature to your faxes – it's easy, and you don't need a scanner

convenient to fax from your word processor – it doesn't have to be Microsoft Word, other programs have built-in faxing facilities or Send and Print commands that will automatically start MS Fax. Write the message, or open the file if you've already written it. If you're not bothering with a cover page, remember to include all relevant details such as your name and fax number in the header. In Microsoft Word 97 you can either click on Send To in the File menu and choose Fax Recipient, which opens another **wizard**, giving you a selection of standard cover pages (Professional, Contemporary or Elegant). Alternatively click on Print on the File menu, and choose Microsoft Fax from the Printer Name drop-down menu and once again you'll be led into the Microsoft Fax **wizard**.

Receiving an incoming fax is equally straightforward. You can elect to answer fax calls manually, in which case double click on the InBox icon on your desktop and minimise the window. When the phone rings – and you are expecting a fax – click on the fax machine icon that appears in the system tray on the Taskbar (next to the time display). This opens a dialogue box; click on the Answer Now button. To enable automatic answer (if you didn't already do so during installation), open Exchange or Messaging and when the InBox window appears, click on Tools, then Microsoft Faxes and Options. Select the **Modem** tab then click on the Properties button. In the box marked Answer Mode there's an option to select auto-answer, and specify the number of rings before pick-up.

Advanced facilities

However, a basic PC-fax setup has one or two shortcomings when compared with a stand-alone fax machine. First, you can only send documents or images created on the PC, and second, you will have to leave the machine switched on, if you want to receive incoming faxes around the clock. So let's look at some ways around those little difficulties and see how you can extend your PC's faxing abilities. Before you begin make sure you have Microsoft Fax installed, set up and working on your Windows 95 PC, as outlined earlier on.

The first thing you will want to do is personalise your fax cover pages or letters, adding your signature or a company logo. It's really easy, and no, you won't need a scanner. Give a friend or colleague a clean copy of your signature or logo and ask them to fax it to you. If possible enlarge the logo on a photocopier and it's a good idea to do a fairly big signature with a thick pen; ordinary handwriting may not come through clearly. Complicated logos may not fare well either, simple designs work best, and small outlines are preferable to large solid patterns, as they will slow your outgoings faxes. When you have the fax on your monitor take a screengrab of the page by pressing Print Screen on the keyboard. Open the Paint program (in the Accessories folder) and edit the image. Trim off any rough edges and clean it up using the paint brushes and eraser tools.

When you're happy with it, click on the Select tool (dotted box), drag an outline box around the logo or signature and select Copy from the Edit menu. Now open the Cover Page Editor, which can be found in Accessories, under Fax. You can either create the cover page from scratch, using the ready-made elements on the Insert menu, or you can modify an existing **template**. If none is shown on the file menu, try looking in the Windows folder. You can drop your graphic in anywhere on the layout by clicking on Paste on the Edit menu. It can be moved around, and if necessary re-sized, using the sizing boxes.

If you have a scanner, or access to one, then so much the better. The fax-it-to-yourself method is only really suitable for simple graphics; a scanner will be able to pick up fine detail or variations in shade on a coloured company logo. In any event a scanner, even a budget model, is a very useful thing to have, especially if you are going to do a lot of faxing from your PC. It means you will be able to send hand-written documents, drawings, even pictures, just like a regular fax machine, and that's quite apart from all of the other things a scanner can do. Quite a few scanners come bundled with dedicated faxing software or utilities, so that once an image has been captured it automatically opens Microsoft Fax, or your default fax program. If not you'll have to save the document as an image file and select it manually, when you start the Fax **wizard**.

Microsoft Fax can be set to auto-answer incoming calls, just like a desktop fax, but what happens when the PC is switched off? A lot depends on the computer's power management facilities – many recent models will respond to a 'wake-up' call from the **modem** whilst the PC is in the Suspend mode. It's not always obvious if a PC is so equipped, in which case you should open Control Panel and click on the Power Icon. If your PC supports these features you should see a button marked Advanced on the Power tab; click on it and put a tick in the check box marked 'Wake up the computer when the phone rings'.

It's also worth checking the PC's **BIOS** settings. This can normally be accessed immediately after the computer is switched on. A message saying something like 'To Enter Set up Press Delete' (or possibly a combination of keys), after which the Set Up screen will appear. Look for a menu option called Power Setting or Management. If the PC supports the Suspend mode there could be an option to enable the wake-up call from the **modem**. If the computer goes into Suspend mode, but doesn't wake up when the phone rings, check the **REN** numbers of all of the devices connected to your telephone line. If the **REN** exceeds 4 this could be preventing the **modem** from picking up the call.

Windows 95 faxing utilities is a very good starting point but it is well worth investigating any bundled software that came with your PC or **modem**. A lot of these programs have additional features, including fax viewers, integrated telephone, smart phonebooks and schedulers.

Finally, some good news if you need to send a lot of faxes abroad and want to avoid running up large international phone bills. Several companies now offer a free or low-cost fax forwarding service over the Internet. You pay only normal on-line and subscription charges. Find out more from Connect International and the Phone Company's web sites at: www.tpc.int/tpc_home.html and http://www.i4l.com/fax/index.htm

Q&A Solutions to real world problems

In or out

Q   I currently have a Pentium 75 home computer and I am very interested in purchasing a **modem** for Internet and e-mail connection. Would you recommend a stand-alone **modem** or one that is integrated within the

computer? Are there any limitations from the somewhat dated computer specification, or is this merely dictated by the **modem** capabilities?
W.M. via e-mail

A   Internal **modems** tend to be a little cheaper, mainly because they do not need a case, serial cable connection or an external power supply, otherwise they're no different to external models. Internal **modems** take up an **ISA** expansion slot and that can be a problem on some recent PCs which have only two slots to begin with. On the other hand, external **modems** monopolise a serial communications port, which are increasingly in demand by other peripherals, including digital cameras, pocket PC docking stations etc. However, in our opinion, the balance tips in favour of an external **modem**, especially when it comes to monitoring your PC's activities. These days a lot of programs have automatic dial-out facilities and with an internal **modem** it's not always obvious if an Internet connection has been made, or terminated. The winking lights on the front of an external **modem** tell you immediately what it's up to, and warn you of any unexpected or unwanted connections. Your PC is perfectly adequate for Internet browsing and most other routine applications, like word-processing etc. The only time it might seem a little slow is with the latest graphics and games software.

Socket sense

Q   I regularly visit a number of European countries. I would like to take my laptop PC and **modem** with me and want to be able to send and receive e-mail and faxes – is there such a thing as a universal phone-socket adaptor?
M.M. London

A   No, there are simply too many variations in socket design. World-wide there are more than fifty types, and counting. You can get **modem** adaptor kits that cater for the most common sockets in Europe, Scandinavia, America and the Far East. However, many seasoned laptop travellers – frustrated by the difficulty of connecting to overseas telephone networks – would not leave home without one far more useful accessory, and that's a screwdriver with which they can hardwire their **modems** into the phone junction box in their hotel rooms. It's not something we could possibly recommend though...

Contact: Avro Modem Adaptor Kit, circa £45 mail order from many PC accessory suppliers.

Nuisance calls

Q How can I deal with irregular, randomly timed phone calls – some as early as 3a.m. – that emanate either from computers or fax machines? When a call occurs we hear beeps but not a continuous tone like a **modem**. We have connected our old fax machine but have not been able to capture a fax. Leaving the phone off the hook is very inconvenient. However, when we get one of these calls, one or more usually follows some minutes later. So we have to leave the phone disconnected in order to get any sleep. Any suggestions please?
B.S. via e-mail

A This is a growing problem, and it's not just caused by wrongly programmed fax machines and **modems**. There are a huge number of automated systems, such as refrigeration units and boilers that use the telephone to send reports or notify faults. Caller ID systems and the 1471 number recall facility often doesn't work as the call may originate from a company PBX system. BT tell us they have a free action plan to deal with this type of call, culminating in a change of number, if they can't track down the offending equipment. Once alerted, via their customer services department (call 150), they will try to trace the number and notify the operator of the equipment. Subscribers can also try the BT Malicious Calls Bureau (freephone 0800 661441), who will deal with this kind of complaint. The Bureau operate a free general advice line on what to do about nuisance calls, on freephone 0800 666700, and leaflets are available from BT shops.

Fire risk?

Q I run fax software and am in the habit of leaving my PC on permanently but with the monitor and printer switched off at night or when I'm on holiday. I have heard stories of PCs blowing up because of power supply defects. Is it safe to leave an unattended PC switched on for an indefinite period?
N.B. via e-mail

A   PC power supplies that conform to current UK and European safety standards are designed to operate continuously and in general they are well protected against overheating and overload. Almost all PC **power supply modules** are housed in ventilated metal enclosures and the chances of anything inside blowing up and causing damage to its surroundings are very small indeed.

Nevertheless, it's worth keeping an eye on any PC running all of the time, and ensure that air can circulate freely around the case. Inspect the area around the **power supply module** and fan grille on a regular basis; no part of a PC should ever be more than slightly warm to the touch and if you detect a sudden rise in temperature a fault could be developing.

Faulty fax

Q   Why won't my Windows 95 software work? I get messages like 'Internal MAPI Error' and 'Unrecoverable Error'. I have tried uninstalling and then re-installing but it still won't work.
B.N. London

A   There is a known problem with Windows 95 OEM service releases 2 and 2.1. The solution is to use Add/Remove in Control Panel to remove all Windows Messaging components, then restart Windows and re-install MS Fax from the CD-ROM. Windows Messaging is added by default. Incidentally, Windows 98 doesn't have the option to install MS Fax from the Add/Remove Programs utility on Control Panel. Instead you have to use Windows Explorer to install a file on the CD-ROM called Wms-exe. It's contained in a folder called Intl, which can be found by opening Tools, then Oldwin95, and Message; this will install Windows Messaging and after that you should return to the Intl folder and click on Awfax.exe.

CHAPTER 14

Spring cleaning

Dust and grime build up alarmingly in a computer and can affect its operation. We explain how you can keep your machine spick and span.

A PC is like a vacuum cleaner, sucking in dirt and debris so you should periodically clean it out using a can of compressed air

In addition to processing words and crunching numbers, your desktop computer does a pretty good impression of a vacuum cleaner and rubbish bin. Cooling fans inside the **power supply module**, and attached to the main processor chip, suck air in through and around the disk drives, loudspeaker grilles and gaps in the cabinet. After just a few weeks' use, everything inside the case is coated with a thin layer of dust particles and airborne contaminants. It gets everywhere and could eventually cause your PC to operate erratically, or worse.

Dust and pollutants can interfere with the pickup heads and other moving parts inside the floppy disk and CD-ROM drives. Intermittent contacts may develop on switches, plugs, sockets, **expansion cards** plugged into the **motherboard**, even the microchips can be affected. The biggest accumulation of dust is in and around the main cooling fan and in extreme cases it can cause the power supply to fail by blocking the path of cooling air to critical components.

The keyboard uses gravity to collect your detritus. A noxious mixture, made up of biscuit crumbs, cigarette ash (even if you don't smoke), nail clippings, hairs and tea and coffee spillage finds its way past the keys and into the inside of the keyboard case. The keys themselves also suffer a build-up of sticky surface grime made up of skin oil, sweat, makeup and other substances. Most PC users seem to favour leaving it, until it gets full up, the keys stop moving or it starts to smell...

Then there's the mouse. They're especially good at keeping the mouse mat clean, hoovering up crumbs, dirt and liquid spills. Debris is transferred from the ball underneath onto the rollers that move optical or mechanical switches. After a while pointer movement becomes jerky, or stops altogether. It's worth mucking out your system at least once a year, more often if you work in a particularly dusty or smoky atmosphere, or if you regularly eat lunch at your desk.

There's really only one way to clean out the system unit, and that's to take off the lid, but remember to disconnect it from the mains before you reach for the screwdriver, and dissipate any static charges that may have built up on you body by touching the case metalwork. Don't be tempted to suck out the dust using the hose on your vacuum cleaner – that's just asking for trouble as you might dislodge cables plugs or **expansion cards**. Instead, get hold of a can of compressed air – the sort used to clean cameras – and blow the dust out of the case. They are also better at getting into nooks and crannies. Most of them have extension tubes, so you can also blast dust out of the power supply and off of the cooling fan blades. Don't poke the tube inside the disk drive slot as you could damage the delicate innards; use proper disk-drive cleaning kits, available from your local computer store.

Before you put the lid back on, you can do a spot of preventative maintenance. If your machine has been in regular use for more than a couple of years it may become prone to a condition known as 'chip creep', which can lead to intermittency or failure. As the **motherboard** heats up and cools down it flexes slightly, slowly pushing microchips out of their sockets. Identify the socket-mounted chips and apply gentle finger pressure to re-seat them.

It's no good trying to shake the dirt out of your keyboard; it just gets trapped underneath the keys. The only solution is to take it apart, but make sure the PC is switched off. Designs vary but most keyboards are held together by half a dozen (or more), crosshead screws on the underside. Once removed, the top and bottom halves should come apart. You may have to prise some small lugs with the tip of a screwdriver but if it doesn't separate easily don't force it! Tip out all of the loose dirt and using a new, soft paintbrush remove all the dirt from underneath the keys. A soft cloth dampened with water and a drop of washing-up liquid will remove the grime coating the keys and exterior surfaces of the case. Dry it off and reassemble, making sure there are no wires trapped between the case sections.

The best way to clean your mouse is to take it apart. If you don't fancy tinkering around inside, it's still worth removing and cleaning the ball, but only when the PC is switched off. The ball is usually held in place by the ring surrounding it. It should drop off when turned a few degrees. Give the ball a wipe over and blow into the hole, to shift any loose dust. Most mice are held together by one or two crosshead screws on the base so you can separate the two halves and clean it out using the paintbrush. Handle with care as the rotary sensors may only be clipped lightly into place and could fall out if the circuit board is turned upside-down. Check the condition of the rollers that come into contact with the ball. If there's a coating of gunge it can be scraped off with a matchstick.

If you're feeling particularly diligent, then sort out the rats-nest of cables on the back of your PC. Untangle the leads, unplugging them one at a time if necessary and making sure the retaining screws on the large multi-pin connectors are tightened up. Plugs working loose are the cause of many problems.

Finally, the monitor. Do not on any account take it apart – this is a no-go area! Very high voltages are present that remain even when it is switched off. Use the can of compressed air to blow dust out of the

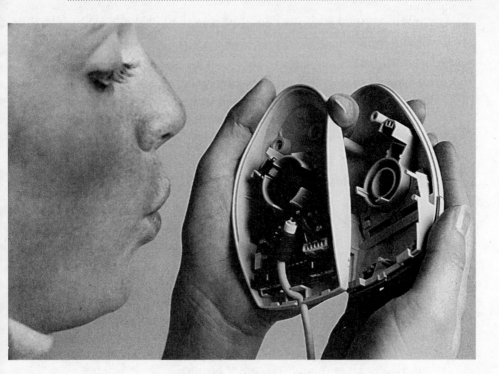

The performance of your mouse will deteriorate if fluff and dirt are allowed to accumulate inside

ventilation slots on the top, bottom and sides. Make sure they're not covered, as this could lead to overheating. Keep the screen clean using purpose-designed anti-static foam cleaner or wipes. Remember that a clean PC is a happy PC!

Q&A   Solutions to real world problems

Key for two

Q   My PC keyboard has begun acting up and several keys have become unreliable, only working if you hit them really hard. Could this have

anything to do with the cup of tea that I accidentally spilt on to the keys a couple of weeks ago?
J.J. Hillsborough

A   You've got it in one, and it's not going to get better. Tea, or any beverage for that matter, leaves behind a sticky residue that interferes with the electrical contacts on the keyboard. It needs to be taken apart and thoroughly cleaned.

Grubby cables

Q   The curly lead connecting my keyboard to the PC, and the mouse lead are absolutely filthy. They were probably white once but now they are black with grime. Can they be cleaned, and if so what is the best way?
S.D. Chepstow

A   Make sure the PC is switched off first, then you can clean the wires with a damp cloth and a little washing-up liquid. It will probably be easier to clean the cables after they have been unplugged. Make sure the cables and plugs are thoroughly dry before they are reconnected; it's best to leave them overnight if possible.

Dirty old ROM

Q   I'm experiencing difficulty with my CD-ROM drive, which has become very unreliable. I keep getting messages, saying the machine cannot read from the drive and I suspect that it may be due to dirt on the pickup. I would like to know if it's safe to use an ordinary audio CD cleaner, or do I need a special kit?
M.L. Honiton

A   The drive and pickup mechanism in a CD-ROM drive is basically the same as those used in audio CD decks, so you can use a regular cleaning kit without any problems, although they may not always remove really stubborn contamination. The fan inside the PC's power supply sucks in air, some of it through the gap around the CD loading tray. Significant amounts of dust can accumulate inside the drive after just a few weeks. There are several purpose-designed CD-ROM cleaners on the market. The Hama Pro-Scan (£14.99) is worth trying, if a regular cleaner doesn't clear the problem. This one has a pair of tiny brushes set into the disk that sweep the lens clean. This particular cleaner also includes software on the disk to test the computer's monitor, sound card and speakers. Contact Hama UK, telephone 01256 708110. The one sold by Tandy (Catalogue No. 26-390) for £9.99, is also worth trying. While you're at it, give the floppy disk drive a wash and brush up as well, they hoover up even more dust than CD-ROM drives.

Safe solution

Q   Is it safe to use cleaner wipes meant for telephones, on my PC keyboard and mouse? I'm wary of using anything that might contain harmful chemicals that attack plastics.
F.P. Dundee

A   PC peripherals and telephones are made from the same family of plastics so it's very unlikely the wipes would contain any damaging solvents, but do check labelling for warnings.

What's the score?

Q   My PC monitor was knocked off my desk and as it fell it struck the corner of a filing cabinet, leaving an inch-long scratch on the glass. Is it possible for this to be removed, and if so, how much is it likely to cost?
G.L.A. via e-mail

A   Unless the scratch is very light, it's there to stay, however your local glazier should be able to advise whether or not it can be removed by polishing. If it is deep it could be potentially dangerous as another blow to the screen could cause the scratch to crack the glass, which would shatter the tube and you don't want to be there when that happens! Play it safe and have it looked at.

Filter tip

Q   I work in the dusty and smelly atmosphere of a furniture manufacturer and I'm fairly sure my PC is slowly filling up with sawdust, which can't

be doing it much good. Do you know of anyone who makes a filter that I could stick over the back of the fan on my computer?
W.W. Sheffield

A   It wouldn't do any good. The cooling fans in PC power supplies suck air in through the slots and gaps in the cabinet, and blow it out the back. There's not much you can do about dust getting into your machine, apart from periodically opening it up and cleaning it out.

CHAPTER 15

Windows 95 tips

*Make your Windows 95 machine run faster and
smoother, customise the desktop and learn some
of the hidden tricks.*

By the right

The right mouse button in Windows 95 has many hidden talents –
here's a few to be getting on with. If you've got a lot of open windows
and you want to get to the desktop, simply right click on the taskbar.
This brings up a menu for minimising, tilting or cascading all
windows, right click on the taskbar a second time to restore the
windows. A right click on the Recycle Bin gives the option to empty it
straight away. Disks can be quickly formatted by right-clicking on the
disk drive icon in My Computer or Explorer.

Better late than never

When you switched on your shiny new PC for the first time, or as
Windows 95 was being installed, you were invited to make an
emergency StartUp disk. Did you? Probably not. It's one of those little
jobs you think you'll get around to later, but inevitably never will. Do
it now! It will only take you a couple of minutes but this simple job
could save you hours of frustration. Click on Start, then Settings,
followed by Control Panel and Add/Remove Programs. You'll find the
tab for the StartUp Disk there, just follow the instructions. That disk
could get you out of big trouble when – as may happen one day –
Windows 95 refuses to run from the hard disk. The disk contains the
necessary files and diagnostic programs, that can get you up and
running once again.

Keys strokes – four worth remembering

Help is always at hand. If you encounter a problem or get into difficulty, just press F1 and the associated Help file will be displayed.
Swapping between open applications in Windows 95 is easy; hold
down the left 'Alt' key and press the 'Tab' key. Pressing Tab again steps
through all of the programs the machine is currently running. If for
any reason a program freezes or the mouse stops moving try pressing
'Alt' and you may find that you can still select menus and options,
using the four arrow cursor keys. If an application refuses to respond,
then press and hold down 'Ctrl', 'Alt' and 'Delete' in that order – once
only – and the PC will display the Close Program window. This gives
the opportunity to shut down the offending application, without
having to exit Windows.

Good mousekeeping

From the Start menu in Windows 95 click on Settings, Control Panel,
and then on the Mouse icon. There you will find a range of settings
that control the way your mouse behaves. There's also the opportunity
to change the button configuration which is useful if you are left-
handed. The two most important parameters for PC newcomers are
Motion and Click Speed; set both to slow and you'll find the mouse
much easier to control. Increase the speed once you get used to how
the mouse reacts. While you're there, click on the Pointers tab and the
Scheme menu, then select the Animated Hourglasses option. This will
make waiting for things to happen just a little more interesting.

Sounds interesting

By now you're probably getting a bit bored with the cheesy tunes,
pings and ta-das coming from your PC, so do something about it! From
the Start menu select Control Panel, and then the Sounds icon. Here
you can find, and change, all the standard sounds, and the actions or
events they're associated with. Click the Browse button or scroll
through the list and you should come across some additional Windows

95 repertoires, called Jungle, Robot and Musica. Try them, they're fun. If they're not there you can load them from the Windows 95 CD-ROM using the Add/Remove programs utility in Control Panel.

The ultimate trick is to make up your own sounds – all you need is a microphone. It plugs into the 'mic' jack socket on the PC's sound card or audio input. It should be on the back of your PC, close to the speaker plug. Find the sound recorder utility, which is in the Multimedia folder in the Accessories directory. It's easy to use, just like an ordinary tape recorder; full instructions are in the associated Help file. When you've recorded your sound, give it a name. From the File menu choose 'Save As' and put it in the Media directory in the Windows 95 folder, then go back to the Sounds icon in Control Panel and assign it to the event of your choice.

Are you sitting comfortably?

Computers can seriously damage your health! Inappropriate seating is a major contributing factor to back pain. If you are going to be seated in front of your PC for more than an hour or so each day, get a proper chair. Purpose-designed office chairs, with adjustable height and back support are ideal, and they're not expensive.

Make sure the screen is at a comfortable height – it should be at eye-level, and that the brightness and contrast are properly adjusted. If you get a lot of reflection on the screen, from bright lights or windows, a clip-on anti-glare screen should help.

Keyboards can cause a lot of problems, especially the cheap ones that come with a lot of PCs these days. Fast typists and those used to mechanical typewriters can find the short, sharp keystrokes of a PC keyboard uncomfortable and it can lead to painful repetitive strain injury or RSI. If you're going to be doing a lot of typing, think about buying an ergonomically shaped keyboard. Wrist support pads can help relieve the strain, but if problems persist you should consult your GP.

Finally, don't sit staring at the screen for hours on end without a break. Stand up from time to time, walk around and you could even try some stretching exercises.

Save power

Your PC and Windows 95 have a number of power-saving features that can help reduce the size of your electricity bill. From the Start button select Settings and then Control Panel, then click on the Power icon, in the Power Management window, select the Advanced option and click OK. Open up the Display icon in Control Panel and select the Screen Saver tab. At the bottom you will see check boxes for the energy saving functions of your monitor. This only works with Energy Star compliant models, but that includes most monitors made in the past couple of years. Set the times for a reasonable period – say 15 to 20 minutes – after which the monitor will go into a low power mode if the PC is idle. The display returns as soon as you move the mouse, or press a key.

Media storage

It doesn't take long to build up a sizeable collection of floppy disks and CD-ROMs. Your PC probably came with half a dozen or more disks, which need to be kept safely, so it's a good idea to get into the habit of looking after them from the beginning. The worst thing you can do is just leave them lying around – they will get lost or damaged.

It's worth investing in some disk storage systems. There are a tremendous variety of racks and stacks designed for audio CDs and they are perfect for CD-ROMs. There's less choice for 3.5-inch floppy disk boxes, but you won't need to get to them so often so they can be tucked away, out of sight. Don't underestimate capacity, especially for CD-ROM storage. It's no good buying a rack for all the disks you have now; they breed like rabbits and you'll quickly run out of space.

Broadly speaking, CD-ROMs and floppy disks survive longest in the kind of conditions we feel comfortable in. They do not fare well in extremes of heat, cold or humidity. CD-ROMs must be kept out of direct sunlight – the plastic will warp and degrade – and the same applies to floppy disks. They must also be stored away from sources of magnetism, which means keeping them well away from loudspeakers, the PC monitor or a TV, electric motors and appliances. Leaving floppy disks and CD-ROMs in their drives won't hurt them, but they may attract dust, which could eventually affect the operation of the drive.

The eyes have it

If you have poor or failing eyesight, computer display screens can be difficult to read. Make sure it is correctly positioned, there is no reflection from lights or windows and that the brightness and contrast settings are properly adjusted. If you find the icons and printing underneath too small to read easily try the Large and Extra Large colour schemes in Display Properties. They're located on the Appearances tab that you can find by double clicking on the Display icon in Control Panel. While you are there, select the Settings tab and try the Larger Fonts size. You may also find it helpful to change the Desktop Area slider to a lower value, especially if it has been set to a high resolution figure (e.g. 1024 × 768 pixels) and you are viewing it on a 14- or 15-inch monitor. Most word processor packages have a 'zoom' facility, to enlarge the size of the text display.

A similar set of options is available from the Accessibility Options icon in Control Panel. Double click the icon to open the window. Select the Display tab, then Settings. The next set of options will enlarge the display, with normal black on white text, or the whole thing can reverse, with white on black characters. Click on Display, then check the Use High Contrast box and confirm the changes by clicking the Apply button. Be patient, it takes a few seconds for the display to change.

Easier volume

You will often find that you want to change the volume of your PC's sound system, however the volume control is not very accessible on a standard Windows 95 installation. Normally most users get to it via the View Menu option in CD Player (click on Start, Programs, Accessories, Multimedia, CD Player, View, Volume Control), but there is a quicker way, and you can have it permanently on the taskbar if you so wish.

From the Start menu, click on Settings, then Control Panel and the Multimedia icon, then select the Audio tab. About halfway down there's a small box marked Show Volume Control on the Taskbar. Check the box and it's done. On the far left side of the taskbar you will see a small loudspeaker symbol; when you click on it a volume slider and mute switch will appear on the screen.

Incidentally, it's a good idea to put the CD Player on the Start menu, if you're in the habit of playing audio CDs on your PC. From the Start menu click on Settings then Taskbar, and select the Start Menu Programs tab. Click on the Add, then Browse buttons and look for the Windows folder. Double click on it to open it up then move the horizontal slider along until the CD Player icon appears. Highlight it, click Open, then Next and select the Start Menu folder at the top of the file tree. To complete, click Next and then Finish.

Start right

You can make your life a lot easier by putting Windows utilities and frequently used programs onto the Start menu. The most useful ones are Windows Explorer, My Computer, Control Panel and CD Player. Start with My Computer, hold on the desktop icon and drag it onto the Start button. Next, open Explorer and double click on the Windows 95 folder, to open it up. Follow the same procedure, by clicking and holding on the CD Player, Explorer and Control Panel icons or folders and dragging them to the Start Button.

For other programs the routine is the same – open the folder, find the icon and move it on to the Start button. If you make a mistake and choose the wrong icon or folder, or you want to remove something from the Start Menu, click on Start, Settings then Taskbar and choose the Start Menu Programs tab. Select the Remove button and scroll through the directory tree until you find the offending item. Highlight it and click the remove button.

If your Start menu becomes overcrowded and icons disappear, check the Show small icons in Start Menu box on the Taskbar Options dialogue box.

Lost and found

In the early days it is easy to lose track of the files you create on your new PC. Come to think of it, it can happen at any time – even experienced users sometimes forget to check what they're doing before clicking on the Save button.

Find is one of the most useful and powerful facilities in Windows 95 and it's readily accessible on the Start menu. If you know the name of the lost file, and roughly where it has been stored, just enter the details. Use the Browse button to narrow down the choice of folders, or search the whole drive. However, if you only remember vague details, such as when it was created, Find can still help. Click on the Date Modified tab and try searching a day or two at a time. Better still, if the file contains text, and you can think of a keyword – preferably one that's not used in any other documents – click on the Advanced tab, and type in the word or words in the Containing Text field. Click on Find Now and off it goes. Double click on any of the files found to open them up.

The right stuff

The right button on your mouse can do some interesting tricks when you're looking at Internet web pages. Click anywhere on the page and you'll see a number of options. The most useful one is to add the address of the current page to your Favourites list. If you come across a background design that you'd like to use as wallpaper on your desktop, right click on the pattern and choose the Set as Wallpaper option. Selecting Copy Background puts the image into the **Clipboard** memory, so you can import it into a graphics program, or it can be filed away as a .gif or .jpg image in the file or folder of your choice, using the Save Background As option.

Theme parks

If you like the idea of being able to drastically change the way your PC looks and behaves, then you don't have to upgrade to Windows 98 or buy any extra software. There are literally thousands of free desktop 'themes' on the Internet, containing wallpaper, sounds and icons linked to almost any subject you care to name. One of the best places to start is the Windows 95 Theme Archive, where you can find everything from exotic animals and sci-fi monsters, to cheesy 60s and 70s sitcoms. The site contains full download and installation instructions, as well as Themes installation software. It can be found at: http://ftp.monash.edu.au//pub/Win95.themes/

Sites for sore eyes

The bright white text area of most word processors can become quite tiring on the eyes after a few hours. You can of course jiggle the brightness and contrast settings on your monitor but a far better solution is to give your blank pages a light grey tint. Open your word processor and load a page of text, so you can judge the effect. Next, from the Start button select Settings, Control Panel and the Display icon. Select the Appearance tab and click in the area marked Window Text. Next click on the Color box and choose the Other option. This will bring up a colour palette, select grey or white from the block of colour options and use the slider to the right of the multicolour panel to adjust the level. Click OK and if necessary re-adjust until you are satisfied with it. The tint only applies to the display and will not affect the way documents look when they are printed.

Dont' be a crash dummy

A common cause of Windows 95 crashes or lock-ups is too many programs running at the same time. You might be lucky and get a warning that something bad is about to happen – a slow-running program is a sign of impending danger – but you can keep an eye on what is happening, and possibly prevent a crash, using a simple utility called the Resource Meter. It is quite well hidden and to find it you should click on the Start button, select Programs, then Accessories and click on System Tools. Double click on Resource Meter and a small bar graph icon will appear on the Taskbar, next to the clock. Placing the mouse pointer over the icon will give you an instant readout of the percentage of resources being used; better still click on it and a set of three bar graphs will appear. Problems can occur when any of the three meters fall below 25%. If that happens you should close one or more programs, not forgetting to save any open files first.

Count easy

If you are using MS Word you've probably discovered Word Count in the Tools menu – don't underestimate it, it may be more versatile than you think. As it stands it will count all of the words in an open document, but if you want to know how many words there are in a paragraph, or block of copy, just use the highlight function, then click on Word Count. You can create a simple keyboard shortcut to Word Count by going to the Tools menu and clicking on Customise. Select the Command tab, highlight Tools in the list of Categories and scroll down the list of Commands until you come to Word Count. Highlight it, then click on the Keyboard button, put the pointer into the Press New Shortcut field and press the mouse button. Decide which keys you are going to use (Ctrl and backslash '\' are usually free) and finish off by clicking Assign and Close.

In the bin

Before Windows 95, when you deleted something on a PC that was it – it stayed deleted, but now there's Recycle Bin, and it lets you change your mind. If you want to reinstate a deleted file, double click on the Bin icon on the desktop, or one of the two you will find in Windows Explorer, either will do. Notice that the icon changes according to whether the bin is empty or not. Highlight the files with the mouse pointer, single click the left mouse button, then from the File dropdown menu click on Restore. Whenever you delete a file or program it's a good idea to wait a day or two, to make sure your PC is behaving normally, before you empty the Bin. If you've deleted files to free up hard disk space, it won't become available until the bin is emptied. You can bypass the Recycle Bin altogether by right-clicking on a file, holding down the shift key and clicking on Delete, or by pressing the Delete button on the keyboard.

Free space

If your hard disk is nearly full and you quickly want to free up some space, you can claw back at least 4.5Mb by deleting unused tutorial animations in Windows Help. Open Windows Explorer, then the Windows folder and double click on Help. Scroll down the list looking for camcorder icons with names like Paste, Scroll, Sizewin, Taskswch and Whatson (they should be listed as Video Clips). Highlight each one in turn and press the Delete key (or right click the mouse button and select Delete). Initially they'll be sent to the Recycle Bin, so the space won't become available until the Bin is emptied.

Sluggish starter

If your Windows 95 PC is starting to get a bit sluggish and files seem to take longer to open, you may be able to pep up its performance with a few simple changes. Open the Control Panel and click on the System icon. Select the Performance tab and click on the File System button. On the Hard Disk tab you will see a box marked Typical Role of this Machine. Change the selection to Network Server. While you're there, make sure the slider marked Read Ahead Optimisation is fully turned up. Click on Apply and re-start your PC.

Printer wisdom

If you have a paper jam do not force it. Always try to remove the blockage in the normal direction of travel and if it tears make sure all of the fragments are removed. If you can't clear the paper path, refer to the manual. Store paper flat in the original packaging and always fan it before loading to free up the sheets and stop them sticking together. If the paper hopper is partially full, always load it so the old paper is used first. Always check to make sure the paper you are using is within the printer's handling limits. Keep printers well away from radiators and out of strong sunlight – especially laser printers – as this can affect print quality.

Clip tricks

The Windows 95 **Clipboard** is a useful way of moving files or blocks of text around and between applications but it can only hold one item at a time and that is lost the next time it is used. There is a handy utility on the Windows 95 CD-ROM, called Clipbook Viewer, which allows you to inspect the contents of the **Clipboard** at any time, and save whatever is in there, for future use. To install Clipbook insert the Windows CD-ROM, open Control Panel, then click on the Install/ Remove icon. Select the Windows Setup tab, click on Have Disk then the Browse button. Assuming drive D: is your CD-ROM, select it and look for a folder called 'Other', in there you will find the clipbook.inf file, select it and follow the dialogue boxes to 'Install'. Clipbook can then be found in the Accessories folder on the Program menu.

Starter motor

Windows Explorer is one of the most useful and important Windows 95 utilities. You probably already have it on your Start menu, (Start, Settings, Taskbar, Start Menu, Add, etc.) but there's an even faster way to get to it, and that's to right click on the Start button, and select Explore. There are several other Explorer keyboard shortcuts worth remembering. Each time you press the Backspace key, Explorer steps back one level up the directory tree. The F2 key allows you to rename a highlighted folder and Shift plus F10 brings up the context based pop-up menu. Clicking once or twice on the Size and Modified headings in the right hand Contents window will sort the files in descending (i.e. largest files or most recently modified first) or ascending orders.

Sounds different

If you are tired of the Windows 95 opening and closing screens, why not change them or create your own? The clouds start-up screen is called logo.sys and can be found in the root of your C: drive. The shut down screens, 'Please wait while etc...' and 'It is now safe...' are called logow.sys and logos.sys; they are filed in the main Windows directory. If you want to keep the originals, rename them or copy and paste them somewhere safe.

You can play around and modify the default images using the Paint program in Windows 95 but you can do a lot more with a graphics program, like PaintShop Pro. If you want to create your own title screens, be aware that the images must be 256 colour bitmap (.bmp) files with dimensions of 320×400 pixels. You can do this by re-sizing a 680×480 pixel image to 320×400. Don't worry if it looks out of proportion (it will be stretched vertically), the image will resume its correct shape when displayed during start-up or shutdown. Remember to save your new pictures as a 256 colour bitmap file, with the correct name and extension (i.e. logo.sys), and make sure you put it back in the right place (i.e. the root of your boot drive), or the Windows 95 folder.

About face

You can easily change the **font** and size of the **typeface** used by Windows 95 for Explorer and icon labelling. It's worth trying if you find it difficult to read, you're using an unusually large or small monitor, or you are simply bored with the default **typeface**. Right click your mouse on an empty space on the desktop and select Properties. When the Display window appears click on the Appearance tab, then in the drop-down menu marked Item, choose Icon. You will then be able to select a new **typeface** from the Font menu.

Screen gem

If you're spending several hours each day staring at your computer's monitor screen, it's important to make sure it is properly set up. Incorrect picture settings can result in fatigue, headaches and eyestrain. Adjusting brightness and contrast by eye can be quite difficult. Monitors also go out of alignment, but some picture faults – such as slowly deteriorating focus, geometry or colour registration is difficult to spot in their early stages. For that reason it's worth periodically checking your monitor with a program such as Ntest. It was created by Nokia's monitor division and features a dozen test patterns, to help you set up your monitor and give it a complete health check. What's more it's free! You can download NTest from the Nokia web site; it is a 1.2Mb zip file, so you will need a decompression utility like WinZip to open it up. Find the details at: http://www.nokia.com/products/ monitors/monitor_test.html and http://www.winzip.com

Strike it lucky

Thunderstorms can occur at any time of the year and can be fatal for PCs. Strikes on nearby overhead cables and sub-stations can send high voltage 'spikes' down mains supplies, frying computers and other electronic devices. It's sensible to switch your PC off, disconnect the mains plug and telephone **modem** lead during a thunderstorm, even if it's not directly overhead. If that's not possible then it is worth investing in surge protection devices, for the mains and telephone connections. Protection devices, built into mains sockets or multi-way adaptors are relatively inexpensive (£20 to £50) compared with the cost of a PC and loss of data. Telephone line protectors start at around £40 and are readily available from PC stockists.

Taken to task

It doesn't take long for the Taskbar at the bottom of the screen to fill up with icons; they get smaller as the number increases and it can be difficult to read the labels. You can easily increase the size of the Taskbar by moving the mouse pointer to the top edge of the Taskbar, where it will turn into a vertical double-headed arrow. Click and hold the left mouse button and you can increase the width of the Taskbar by dragging it upwards; it can be expanded to fill half of the screen if necessary. Clearly this takes up more room on the desktop, so make the Taskbar disappear until it is needed. Click on the Start button, then Settings and Taskbar and check the Auto Hide option. From now on the Taskbar will only be shown when the mouse pointer is at the bottom of the screen.

Device advice

If any of the peripherals attached to your Windows 95 PC are behaving erractically, or not at all, your first port of call should be the Device Manager. This can be found in Control Panel; double click on the System logo and select the Device Manager tab. This will bring up a list of the devices used by, and connected to your machine. If any of the entries has a yellow exclamation mark next to them this could indicate that the source of the problem is a missing or corrupt **driver**. Start the Trouble-Shooter utility by clicking on Help on the Start menu, then type 'Conflict' in the Index field. Double click on the highlighted line that appears and follow the instructions.

Random mouse

In Word 97 there's a useful unpublished facility called Random Word. Every so often you might want to create a block of text quickly, to test out your faxing or e-mail facilities, or produce dummy text to check a page layout. You can of course copy and paste text from another document but Random Word is far quicker. Simply type in the following: '=rand()' and press Return. Word will then generate three paragraphs, each containing the sentence 'The quick brown fox jumps over the lazy dog', five times. You can alter the number of paragraphs and sentences by inserting numbers into the brackets. For example, =rand(6,8) generates a text block of 6 paragraphs, each containing 8 sentences.

Wandering disks

When you make changes to your system, you will often be asked to load the Windows 95 CD-ROM, but can you find it? It's a well-known fact that CD-ROMs grow legs at night and go walkabout. Rather than play hunt the disk, why not copy the essential files on your hard disk? They're contained in a folder called Win95. It's not as large as you might think; only around 40Mb on early versions, rising to 125Mb on the later releases, which is relatively small beer on a multi-gigabyte hard disk drive. Open Windows Explorer and create a new folder in the C: drive called Win95. Highlight the Win95 folder on the CD-ROM and click on Copy on the Edit menu, then open the empty Win95 in drive C: and click Paste on the Edit menu and the files will be copied across. The next time your PC asks you to insert the Windows 95 CD-ROM simply change the drive path from D:\Win95 to C:\Win95.

Fatter floppies

Every so often you may want to transfer files between PCs on floppy disk. It's no problem, providing the file is no larger than 1.4Mb. If it is you could compress the data, or use multiple floppies, but there's another option, which is to compress the disk. Windows 95 has a utility called DriveSpace. It is intended to increase the capacity of hard disk drives, but it works just as well with floppies, almost doubling their capacity, to around 2.6Mb. Insert a clean disk into drive A: and from the Start Menu click on Programs, Accessories then System Tools and open DriveSpace. Click on the disk icon or choose compress from the File menu and follow the instructions.

CHAPTER 16

Upgrading to Windows 98

The latest version of Windows is now supplied as standard with a lot of new PCs. Isn't it time you upgraded?

Should you stick with the devil you know, or upgrade to Windows 98? That's the question a lot of Windows 95 users have been asking themselves over the past few months. Now that it is here you have the chance to actually do something about it, although if you're about to buy a PC it may not be an option. From now on most new PCs will come with Windows 98 as standard, but what about the rest of us?

There is no simple answer. For many PC users Windows 98 has genuine advantages, for others it could be the start of a long, horrible nightmare. We'll take a brief look at the highlights and pitfalls, and later on we'll run through the installation and set-up procedures.

First the basics. Windows 98, like Windows 95, is a PC **operating system** – a sophisticated piece of software that controls the way a PC works, provides a platform for other programs and a user-friendly, mouse-clicking interface for you. According to the blurb the minimum configuration for Windows 98 is a PC with a 486 or faster processor, 16Mb of **RAM** and 195Mb of free hard disk space. Roughly translated that means don't bother unless you've got a moderately fast Pentium (133MHz plus). 16Mb **RAM** is an absolute minimum – you'll need 32Mb for comfort – and if you want to be on the safe side make sure you have at least 400Mb to 500Mb of free space on your hard drive.

The Windows 98 upgrade disk is currently selling for around £60 to £70. In the scheme of things that's not an unreasonable price for such a large and sophisticated lump of software, so we're off to a fairly good start. Unlike the change from Windows 3.x to Windows 95 you won't have to learn any new tricks. Windows 95 and 98 are very similar in appearance and all of your existing icons, shortcuts, desktop settings and sounds are preserved in the changeover. There's plenty of extra bits and bobs, and it has borrowed a lot of features from the Internet, but most of them can be ignored, or hidden so that everything looks and feels reassuringly familiar.

If you install Windows 98, hate it, or something goes wrong during or after the installation, then you should be able to return to your original Windows 95 set-up, provided you allow the installation program to make the necessary backup files. That's the theory anyway.

There is a point of no return however. When the installation has finished, Windows 98 will ask you if you want to reorganise your hard disk drive. Don't panic, it's not compulsory, you can say no or do it later. This option changes the way files are stored on the disk drive. The system used on Windows 3.x and the original release of Windows 95 is called **FAT** 16. This is quite wasteful of space and there are problems with hard drives 2Gb or larger. Later versions of Windows 95 and Windows 98 use the more efficient **FAT** 32 system. If you decide to convert, it will almost certainly claw back several tens, possibly hundreds of megabytes of wasted space on your drive. It should also mean that some programs open and run faster. However, once you have converted to **FAT** 32 you can't go back.

The most obvious difference between Windows 95 and 98 is the extensive use of Internet-style **browser** windows. Internet access is a core feature and Internet Explorer 4 is installed on your machine whether you like it or not. It shouldn't affect your existing Internet software, unless you want to replace it. Windows utilities have a more uniform appearance and most of them contain extra, helpful information but the familiar elements – icons and menus – remain the same. There are hypertext links all over the place (highlighted and underlined key words) and if you click on them Explorer will try to dial up an Internet connection. This can be annoying, especially if your PC isn't connected to the Internet, so be careful where you point your mouse. The good news is that existing software on the PC is unaffected by the change.

Future proofing could be a big selling point for Windows 98. It supports a wide range of hardware and software developments, including **USB** and **FireWire** interfaces, for the next generation of peripherals and digital devices. It is ready and waiting for Web TV services – there are many multimedia enhancements to make games run faster, and there's the facility to use two or more monitors.

Microsoft is claiming that Windows 98 is more stable than its predecessor and on the evidence so far, that does seem to be the case. A lot of bugs have been fixed (there were apparently, more than 3,000), moreover the new software comes with advanced diagnostic and problem-solving utilities. It also has a very useful disk cleanup program, to get rid of unused or unwanted files, and you can schedule overnight disk **defragging** to keep files in good order. However, no one is guaranteeing a smooth ride and there are plenty of early adopters with tales of woe to tell. The trouble is there's no easy way to predict how a particular machine will behave. If your PC has long-standing conflicts or glitches that conventional trouble-shooting techniques and cleanup software have failed to sort out and you're reaching the end of your tether, Windows 98 could be worth trying.

On balance, Windows 98 appears to be a genuine improvement over Windows 95. If you're about to buy a new PC it is definitely worth having. As for existing users, the jury is still out. If your machine is getting a bit wheezy, the hard disk is filling up and you're experiencing more frequent crashes, it might solve some problems. It does a lot of things better than Windows 95 and there are lots of new toys to play with; dabblers and fiddlers are going to love it. However, if your present machine is behaving itself and meeting all of your present needs then the devil you know is still your safest bet, at least for a little while longer.

Installing Windows 98

Having taken the decision to upgrade to Windows 98, the first thing to do, before you even think about taking the CD-ROM out of its cover, is back up all of your data files on a removable disk or tape. That means making a copy of everything you've created on your computer, from word processor documents and accounts to your Internet address book and e-mail. In fact anything that cannot be easily replaced, just in case the installation goes belly-up.

From what we know of Windows 98 so far, the chances of it being responsible for an irrecoverable disaster during the installation is very small indeed, but there's no point in tempting fate. The process can easily take a couple of hours which is plenty of time for all sorts of unexpected things to happen. Choose the time you carry out the update carefully, set aside an afternoon, evening or weekend and whatever you do, don't attempt it on a busy work day – that's just asking for trouble.

Although Windows 98 thoroughly checks your machine before, during and after the installation, now is a good time to put right any small glitches and get rid of any dead wood. Open Windows 95 Explorer and run through all of the programs that you have. Remove any you no longer need using the Add/Remove facility in Control Panel or the program's own uninstaller. Make sure that you have at least 200Mb of free space on the hard disk before you begin.

Close down all running programs in Windows 95, insert the Windows 98 CD-ROM and it should start automatically. If not, then click on Run in the Start menu and select SetUp, or double click on the CD-ROM icon on My Computer and choose SetUp from there. The opening screen tells you what it is going to do, and roughly how long it will take. This depends on the speed of your PC, the size of the **RAM**, the size of the hard drive, and how full up it is. During the initial stages you may or may not be asked to run **Scandisk**, or rather it will run it for you. The installer will also ask you if you want to back up all of your Windows 95 files, so you can return to your original configuration. You would be unwise not to!

Hopefully the installation will go smoothly. You don't need to stand over it, but keep an eye on it as you will have to make some decisions from time to time. It might suggest switching off or updating any anti-virus software you're using (some programs may object to Windows 98) and whether or not to make an emergency recovery disk (do it!). You will need a blank formatted floppy disk for that, so have one handy. It will ask which type of installation you want (typical, portable, custom or compact), and you'll have to enter a few details concerning you, your PC and Internet connectivity.

Eventually, after the PC has re-booted for the last time you will be asked for a password. If you're the only one using it just ignore it, after that you'll see the Welcome screen and you're ready to go. At this point you will be invited to register the program via the Internet, take a guided tour, or go straight to the Maintenance **wizard**.

It's worth spending a few minutes with the tutorial but if you decide to press on then you should see your old familiar desktop, but with a few extra icons and elements. One obvious difference will be the way the Start menu is organised. There will be two new entries: Favourites and Log Off. Favourites is a collection of frequently accessed folders and Internet web sites. If you click on a document, Windows 98 launches your word processor, selects an image file, takes you straight to a graphics application, and so on. The integration of web browsing facilities in Windows 98 is immediately obvious. If you point your mouse at an Internet-related entry, the address appears and if you click on it Win 98 dials it up for you, automatically logging on to your ISP (Internet Service Provider) and connecting to the relevant site. Log Off is a facility that allows several people to share the PC and access their own customised desktop, without having to close Windows every time.

Many Windows 98 features look and work differently, although if you've installed Internet Explorer 4.0 some of it will already be familiar. My Computer, Control Panel and Explorer are typical examples; they are contained inside **browser**-style windows and resemble web pages in appearance. It is designed to make it easier to move around and organise files and fortunately the changes are quite subtle and you quickly get used to them. Settings on the Start menu contain a utility called Folder options that switches between web-type single click file/folder open and conventional Win 95 double-click actions.

Of more immediate interest are the customising options contained in a new Control Panel item called Themes (previously seen on the Windows 95 Plus pack). It comes as standard with Windows 98 and it contains a big collection of wacky Windows wallpapers, backgrounds, pointers, screen savers, sounds and icons. Don't bother unless you've got 32Mb of **RAM** and leave it alone if you want to get any work done, but if you've got an hour or three to spare there's some tremendous fun to be had. On a more serious note, if you have any disabilities, Windows 98 has improved Accessibility Options (also in Control Panel), including a simple screen magnifier to assist those with impaired vision.

The Maintenance **wizard** is a collection of tools, some of them familiar, like the **Disk Defragmenter**, others, such as Disk Cleanup are new to Windows 98. This seeks out and identifies unused or unwanted files and offers to delete them. **Defragging** speeds up disk access but it can take a long time on a large disk drive. Windows 98 can do it automatically, at a time of your choosing, though you have to leave the machine switched on if you do it overnight.

If you've upgraded from Windows 3.1 or the early version of Windows 95, there's the option to convert to the **FAT** 32 disk drive filing system. This is definitely worth doing as in addition to recovering wasted hard disk space, programs will load faster but be warned that once the change has been made, it can't be undone and you won't be able to revert to your previous installation.

We've barely scratched the surface of Windows 98. Some features, like the Internet tools, troubleshooting utilities, multi-display and support for new generation hardware each deserve more attention. However, the key point is that upgrading to Windows 98 is relatively safe and painless and on the evidence so far, a worthwhile exercise.

When Windows 98 goes wrong

Thus far we've been fairly chipper about Windows 98, and it does seem that for the majority of users, upgrades and new installations proceed without incident. When it works it works well, and it does appear to be more stable than its predecessor but web watchers may have noticed that not everyone is jumping for joy.

High on the list of early malcontents are several PC makers, notably Compaq, Dell and Toshiba, who have already expressed doubts about the new **operating system**. Most of the problems concern a lack of drivers, or incompatibility with the **BIOS** on some of their PCs. Compaq has warned their customers of a number of faults. One of the most serious involves the CD-ROM drives on Presario models, which do not work in the **DOS** mode. Several Dell Latitude notebook machines (CP, Cpi, XpiCD and LM) require upgrade files before Windows 98 will behave itself, and owners of Toshiba PCs with ACPI **BIOS** have reported **registry** conflicts. Microsoft and the manufacturers concerned all seem to be working hard to resolve the problems. You can find more information, and where applicable, software patches and workarounds, on their Internet web sites (see below for details).

Windows 98 installations have also been running into trouble on PCs with large and untidy **registry** files. The **registry** can become littered with fragments and clutter, particularly on machines where a lot of programs are installed, and subsequently deleted. Fans of magazine cover-mounted CD-ROMs take note. Anyone thinking about upgrading should also heed our previous warnings about backing up essential files before starting the installation, and saying yes to the option to back up Windows 95, so the original configuration can be recovered, if anything goes wrong.

Even when the installation has apparently gone smoothly there can still be difficulties, and there are plenty of stories doing the rounds on the Internet about the failure of Windows 98 to recognise certain peripherals. **Modems**, scanners and printers seem to be the worst hit. It's a little too early to say if this affects particular brands more than others but it's worth checking the web sites of any manufacturers whose products you're using. These types of faults tend to be less serious and in a lot of cases can be resolved by the Add/Remove hardware utility in Control Panel.

That brings us to the wider subject of what to do if an application or Windows 98 throws a wobbly. Help is always a good place to start when something goes wrong and the new design on Windows 98 makes it easier to find your way around. Incidentally, this is the first major change to Help since the original release of Windows 1.0 in 1983. The new Help works like an Internet web page, with underlined links to other related topics, and direct access to the KnowledgeBase, on the Microsoft web site (assuming it's not the **modem** that has stopped working). There you will find the most up-to-date information and reports concerning Windows 98 and other MS products, that could be connected with your problem. Like earlier versions of Help it will also open folders and launch utilities from within Control Panel and Explorer.

The first place to go for any obvious hardware-related conflicts is Device Manager. It looks much the same as the one in Windows 95 and can be found by clicking on the System icon in Control Panel. Problems with drivers are flagged up with yellow exclamation marks. You can have a go at solving obvious faults by deleting and re-installing corrupt or misbehaving **driver** software. There's the same set of options for delving deeper into the netherworld of DMAs, IRQs and memory resources. However, unless you know what you are doing, it's a good idea to leave them well alone.

There are several new trouble-shooting and diagnostic utilities designed to make it easier to pinpoint software disorders. They can be found in the Accessories folder under System Tools. The most useful one is System Information, which gathers together key data about your computer. The opening window gives a very complete picture of the PC including a nifty 'Uptime' meter that shows how long it has been in use. The left side of the screen provides a close up view of the PC's hardware, external components and software; it's fairly heavy going for non-specialists but those familiar with the innards of their machines will find it invaluable.

The Tools menu on System Information launches a set of handy problem-solving utilities. Windows Report collects data and records critical system files, for backup and scrutiny by engineers, if it needs expert attention. System File Checker does just that, scanning all of the computer's critical files for errors. Registry Checker inspects that vital and mysterious folder for glitches and there's a new version of Dr Watson, for diagnosing tricky faults. System Configuration Utility zooms in on the all-important start-up files, including autoexec.bat, config.sys, system.ini, win.ini and startup. They may not mean a lot to you if you're new to PCs but alongside each line of gobbledegook text there's a reassuring tick box, that confirms all's well, or not, as the case may be. Finally, on the Tools menu there's a short cut to **Scandisk**, which checks the integrity of the hard disk drive and its file structure, and Version Conflict Manager, which keeps an eye out for files that are likely to disagree with one another.

The upshot of all this is that Windows 98 is well equipped to deal with problems, and it should make it easier to find the causes, although not necessarily the cures. However, it's still early days and only time will tell if we can expect the same fun and games we had with Windows 95.

Contacts

http://www.compaq.com
http://www.dell.com
http://www.toshiba.com
http://microsoft.com

Glossary

8mm

Video and data recording system using 8mm wide magnetic tape. The cassettes are roughly the size of an audio cassette.

Alignment

Spaces between words can be microscopically adjusted so that text completely fills each line – this is known as justified text. If standard sized word spacing is used, each line will have a variable length; this is called 'ragged'. A column with ragged lines on the right side is 'aligned left' or 'ranged left'; if the left side is ragged it is 'ranged right'. Centred text is ragged text that is symmetrically opposed about a notional line running down the middle of the column.

BIOS

Basic Input Output System. This is a set of instructions that tells your PC what it is connected to, and how to communicate with devices like the hard disk drive and memory chips.

Browser

Internet access program, such as Microsoft Internet Explorer or Netscape Navigator. A browser provides an easy to use 'window' on the Internet, and other types of computer network locating and displaying various types of graphic and text information.

Cache

A section of computer memory set aside for storing frequently-used data from a disk drive, speeding up the transfer of information.

CCD

Charged Coupled Device. A microchip image sensor that converts light into digital data.

Chip Sockets

Most of the microchips used in a PC are soldered directly to the circuit boards but some, including the main processor and some memory components, are mounted in sockets, so they can be easily replaced or upgraded.

Clipboard

Clipboard is a section of a computer's memory where you can temporarily copy chunks of text, data, graphics or pictures. Once on the clipboard the item can be pasted into another part of the document, or transferred to any other application running on the PC that has a copy and paste facility.

Clip Art

Copyright-free pictures, icons and cartoons supplied with word processor programs, or available separately, that can be used to illustrate documents.

Compression

A technique to reduce the size of a file in order to make it more manageable and faster to download. Compressed files have to be extracted with a utility such as WinZip. Zipped files usually have the extension .zip.

Consumables

Components such as the ink cartridge or ribbon in a printer that need to be replaced when it runs out, or exceeds its life expectancy.

Cookies

Small data files created by an Internet web site and stored on the user's PC. A cookie contains information that can help speed access on subsequent visits, such as passwords, details of the PC's display capabilities and, if supplied, the user's e-mail address.

Cropping

Trimming the edge of an image, so that it fits the space allocated.

Daisywheel

A type of 'impact' printer. Characters are mounted on a spinning wheel and stamped on to an inked ribbon in order to leave an impression on a sheet of paper.

DAT

Digital Audio Tape. A high quality recording system using small matchbox-sized tape cassettes spooled with 4mm wide magnetic tape.

Defragging

Over time the files on a PC's hard disk drive become disorganised. 'Defragging' the drive with a disk defragmenter restores order and speeds up reading and writing data.

Desktop Publishing (DTP)

Desktop publishing programs are designed with page layout in mind.

The emphasis is on moving and manipulating text, graphics and photographs, though pretty well all of them have word processing facilities as well.

DIMMs

Dual In-Line Memory Module. A small circuit board that plugs into the main PC motherboard, containing a number of memory chips.

Disk Defragmenter

See Defragging.

DOS

Disk Operating System. A software program that tells a computer how to control and communicate with devices like disk drives, memory chips and the various input and output connections or 'ports'.

Dot Matrix

A type of impact printer. Characters are built up by a row of tiny moving print heads that stamp dots on to the paper, via an inked ribbon.

Driver

Drivers are small programs that tell Windows 95 how to communicate with a particular piece of hardware, like a mouse, joystick or printer.

DVD/DVD-RAM

Digital versatile/video disk. High capacity optical disk system, using 12cm disks. DVD-RAM is the name for recordable DVD machines.

EDO-RAM

Extended Data Out, Random Access Memory. High-speed RAM chips used on recent PCs with specialised memory controllers.

EISA/ISA

Extended Industry Standard Architecture. A type of connector on a PC motherboard, used for expansion or adapter cards.

Emergency Recovery Disk

If Windows fails to boot up, the Emergency Recovery Disk contains the necessary start-up files to get it running, along with troubleshooting and diagnostic utilities.

Encryption

A process that turns files into gobbledegook so they cannot be read, other than by programs containing the appropriate password-protected de-cryption software.

Expansion Cards

Most PCs contain a set of small circuit boards, or expansion cards, plugged into the main motherboard, for controlling the video output, processing sounds or communicating with the outside world (modems and network cards).

Extensions

Files are identified by a three or four letter or number code, called an extension, that comes after the full-stop following the filename. Common types include .doc and .txt for word-processor documents. Files ending in .bmp and .jpg generally contain images. Files ending in .exe or .com usually contain executable programs which load into the memory and carry out a set of instructions, as opposed to a passive data file that contains data or information; .sys files are mostly used for driver software, used by the PC to communicate with hardware devices.

FAT

File Allocation Table. The part of a PC's disk system that decides how and where disk storage space is allocated.

File Fragments

When programs are removed from a hard disk, bits of files often get left behind. Scandisk checks to make sure they're not associated with existing programs and converts them to complete files so they can be safely deleted.

FireWire

(Aka IEEE1394) A high speed communications link for connecting PCs to digital video and audio devices.

Font/Typeface

Text style and size. Virtually all word processors have a 'wizzywig' display (actually WYSIWYG, or What You See Is What You Get), so what appears on the screen is what ends up on the printed page.

Freeware

Shareware programs that are free to use, but the author retains control of the original code.

Host

An Internet company providing storage space for web sites on their server computer.

HTML

HyperText Mark-up Language. Hidden text-based codes and commands on a web page, which help your browser to move around documents and access other sites.

Hyperlink
Coloured and underlined text, or graphics that if clicked on will take you to another part of a document, web site or different web site altogether.

Gameport
A 15-pin female connector socket designed exclusively for joysticks and other control devices.

Inkjet
Type of printer. Images are built up by tiny drops of ink, squirted from a moving print head or cartridge, onto paper. Most colour inkjet printers use a mixture of cyan, magenta and yellow inks, sometimes with black, to produce a full range of colours.

JPEG
Joint Photographic Experts Group. A subcommittee of the International Standards Organisation, responsible for devising software compression systems. It is a picture file format used for storing photographs. Data is compressed, thus saving space and reducing download times on Internet pages.

Modem
Modulator/DEModulator. A device that converts digital signals coming to or from your PC into audible tones that can be sent via a conventional telephone line.

Motherboard
The main printed circuit board inside a PC, containing the main processor chip (486, Pentium etc.), memory chips (RAM), plus all the other circuits needed to control the disk drives, keyboard etc., and communicate with plug-in expansion cards.

Nag Screen
A dialogue box that opens before the main program to remind you to register and pay.

OCR
Optical Character Recognition. Software that translates a scanned image of printed or typewritten text into a plain text file that can be read by a word processor.

On-Line Banking

Most banks will now allow you to operate your account by telephone and some (notably Barclays, Nationwide, National Westminster and Royal Bank of Scotland) are experimenting with direct PC connection, via the Internet.

Operating System

The operating system or OS is a program, or collection of programs that manages all of your PC's resources – RAM, disk-drives, display screen etc. – and controls how files are stored and retrieved.

Packet

Digital data on the Internet is conveyed in short bursts, which help maximise the capacity of the high-speed telephone lines and communications links between server computers.

PC card

(Short for PCMCIA – Personal Computer Memory Card International Association.) It is a standard-sized module used in laptops for memory expansion and other peripherals, including modem cards.

PCI

Peripheral Component Interconnect. Type of connector on PC motherboards, used for expansion or adapter cards.

POST

Power On Self Test. A small diagnostic program that operates every time you switch your PC on, to make sure everything is working correctly.

Power Supply Module

The power supply module converts mains electricity into a low voltage DC, needed by the motherboard and disk drives. It's normally housed inside a metal box which is fitted with a cooling fan, attached to the back of the case or system unit.

Public Domain Software

Shareware programs that are free to use and modify as the author has relinquished control over the code.

QIC

Quarter Inch Committee. Standards organisation responsible for devising data storage system, using quarter-inch wide magnetic tape.

RAM

Random Access Memory. A computer's working memory, where programs store information when they are running. The bigger it is, the less time your computer will have to wait to get data from the hard disk drive.

Registry

A large, constantly changing file in Windows 95, containing details of how your PC is set up, and all the programs stored on the hard disk.

REN

Ringer Equivalence Number. All devices (modems, fax machines, answering machines etc.) that can be connected to the public switched telephone network (PSTN) are required to have a REN number. This determines how many other devices can be connected to the same line. Most phone lines can support a REN of 4. If it is any higher, some devices may not function correctly.

Resizing

Changing the physical size of an image or object on the page, usually by dragging a sizing square, so that it fits into a space.

Ribbon Cable

Flat multi-way cable, used inside a PC to connect disk drives to the main motherboard or plug-in controller.

Scandisk

A Windows utility that checks the integrity of data stored on a hard disk drive, identifies problems, and where possible, puts them right.

SCSI

Small Computer System Interface or 'scuzzy'. A high-speed data interface that uses a card, which plugs into an ISA (integrated system architecture) socket on the PC motherboard. SCSI cards that use PCI (peripheral component interconnect) slots are also available.

Search Engine

An Internet site that works like an interactive telephone directory. Web sites can be found by entering keywords or simple phrases that the search engine uses to seek out information. The search results may contain several hundred, or even thousand 'hits' containing a short summary. To access the site, the user simply clicks on the highlighted text.

Sectors

Hard disk drives are split into tracks and sectors, which is a way for the PC to identify where particular files or pieces of data are stored.

SDRAM

Synchronous Dynamic Random Access Memory. Another family of memory chips that allows data to be accessed at higher speeds.

SIMM

Single In-line Memory Module. With 30 or 72 connecting pins.

Shareware

Software programs that you can try before you buy. If you decide to use it you should send a payment to the author or publisher.

SPAM

Junk e-mail. And yes, it can be just as annoying as the stuff that comes through your letterbox.

Spool

Simultaneous Peripheral Operations On-Line. A way of maximising PC and printer efficiency. Information to be printed is transferred to a temporary file, so the PC can get on with other jobs, and carry on printing when it has a moment to spare.

Standby

PCs with motherboards that support the Standby function, switch to a low power mode when the Standby function is engaged. A variety of actions, including mouse clicks, key presses, or signals from the modem wakes up the PC.

Templates

A ready-prepared document layout. Microsoft Word has lots to choose from, including simple personal letters, fax headers, memos and invoices. To customise them to your own needs simply change the sample text.

TSR

Terminate and Stay Resident. These are programs that load automatically into the computer's memory and operate in the background until needed.

TWAIN

Technology Without An Important Name. An industry-standard software utility that operates in the background, acquiring an image from a scanner or digital camera.

URL

Uniform Resource Locator. A standard Internet address e.g. http://www.telegraph.co.uk

USB

Universal Serial Bus. Industry standard connection system for peripherals (modems, joysticks printers etc.) that does away with confusing technicalities and enables 'hot swaps', allowing connection and disconnection with the PC switched on.

Video Grabber

Device used to convert a video image from a camera or VCR into a form that can be viewed and processed by a PC.

Wizard

A self-activating program that guides you through a simple set-up routine for a particular feature or application.

ZIF

Zero Insertion Force. Socket fitted to PC motherboard that allows microprocessor chips to be swapped or upgraded.

Zip

Type of compressed file that requires a special program (Pkunzip, WinZip etc.) to expand or decode file.

Index